ASIA REORIENTED

ASIA REORIENTED

A New Conception
of World History

OKAMOTO Takashi

Translated by Michael House

Japan Publishing Industry Foundation for Culture

Note to Readers

This book follows the Hepburn system of romanization for Japanese, the Pinyin system for Chinese, and the McCune-Reischauer system for Korean. Japanese, Chinese, and Korean personal names are written in conventional order: family name followed by given name. Personal titles and ages of public figures mentioned in this book are as of the publication date of the Japanese edition. Macrons have been omitted entirely from the text. Long vowels in reference citations are rendered as single letters rather than double letters, except for "ei."

Asia Reoriented: A New Conception of World History
Okamoto Takashi. Translated by Michael House.

Published by
Japan Publishing Industry Foundation for Culture (JPIC)
2-2-30 Kanda-Jinbocho, Chiyoda-ku, Tokyo 101-0051, Japan

First English edition
Ebook: March 2022
Hardcover: June 2022

Originally published in Japanese under the title *Sekaishi josetsu: Ajia shi kara ichibo suru* by Chikumashobo Ltd. in 2018.
English publishing rights arranged with Chikumashobo Ltd.

Book design: Miki Kazuhiko, Ampersand Works
Jacket and cover image: Painting by Zhao Mengfu, Ming period (National Palace Museum, Taipei)

Printed in Japan
ISBN 978-4-86658-220-7
https://www.jpic.or.jp/

CONTENTS

What Constitutes World History for Most People/The West: Universal and World History/Approaches toward a Global History/Eurocentrism/National History, Japanese History, and Eastern History/East and West/The East-West Differential/History as Seen from an Asian Standpoint/World History as Understood by the Japanese

The Present State of Eastern Historical Studies/The Eastern Historical Studies Bottleneck/A Fresh Look at Periodization/A Fresh Look at the History of East-West Interactions/Pioneering Conceptions/Where to Start/Regions within Asia/What Is the Silk Road?

The Beginnings of Civilization/How Nomadism Figures in the Scheme of Things/The Composition of Civilization/The Ancient Near East/Greece, Rome, and India/From Central Asia to China

Ages of "Collapse"/Climatic Cooling/New Structures/Age of Religion and Faith/"World Religions"?/Christianity, Rome, and the Ancient Near East/East Asian Buddhism

Regime Systemization/East-West Expansion/The Second Stage/Hülegü's Western Conquests/Khubilai's Usurpation

Figure in the Scheme of Things/The Netherlands/The Atlantic Economic Sphere/ Quantitative Expansion/The Advent of Great Britain/England's Dawn/Rule of Law, Anglo-Saxon Style/A Coherent Nation

The Industrial Revolution/The British Empire and the Marshaling of Revolu- tion/The Modern World Economy and Its Core/The Expansion of Credit and the Emergence of Investing/Imperialism and the Present Age/Great Divergence, Great Convergence/"The European Miracle"/Empires in the East and Rule of Law/Empires in the West and the Middle Ages

"The Middle Ages" and "the Modern Era"/The Modern Era and Historical Studies/The Existence of a Middle Age: China and Japan/The Japanese, His- torical Studies, and Japanese History/The Archipelago up to Early Modern Times/"Great Development": Advance and Standstill/A Socioeconomic Con- version/Japanese History, Asian History, and Europe/Modern Japan and the Present-Day World

PREFACE TO THE ENGLISH EDITION

Japanese people are sensitive to what is happening in the wider world. This may be because, living in the Far East as they do, they realize that Japan is an underdeveloped country relative to other world centers, beyond the reach of civilizing influences. Accordingly, they built their civilization and culture through the national character of admiring and mastering that which comes from abroad.

This Japanese historical process can also be applied to the field of historiography. Japanese have traditionally been fond of the history of China, as it once seemed the be-all and end-all of the world beyond Japanese shores. Then, beginning in the nineteenth century, Japan commenced studying the history of the West, which had come to rule the world by then. Following the Meiji Restoration of 1868, the field of historical studies was instituted—making history an academic subject in Japan—from studies called *kokushi* (national [Japanese] historical studies), *Toyo shi* (Eastern historical studies), and *Seiyo shi* (Western historical studies).

As a systematized modern academic subject, this field of historical studies was itself imported as something more rigorous than the reading of classical Chinese texts that had constituted historical studies in pre-modern Japan. In this field, Japanese history bore the burden of being the "national history" of Japan. Thus, histories of countries other than Japan constituted Western history and Eastern history. Japan is unique in beginning the study of histories of other countries by categorizing them in the aforementioned manner.

As mentioned above, the Japanese started out by studying the history of China and the rest of East Asia, the region in their immediate vicinity, by means of classical Chinese texts. They then absorbed Western history studies as part of an accumulated learning about East Asian history. Therefore, they were unable to accept at face value what was called "world history" in Western history studies. This was because what was called "world history" at the time meant only the history of Europe and North America—the West—disregarding the greater part of Asia, including China.

The Japanese thereupon redefined what Westerners were calling "world history" as "Western history," and having done so, constructed a corresponding "Eastern history" to include the histories of Asian countries that had been omitted from the preexisting "world history." Using methods of historical study that originated in the West, the Japanese restated the historical record as seen in classical Chinese texts which they had been studying up until the Meiji period.

Up to this time, there had never been such an academic field, and it was imagined as the history of the Eastern half of the whole world. The spatial scope initially encompassed by "Eastern history" indicated the history of the lands east from the Pamirs and north from the Himalayas, with China at its heart. Geographically, this would be roughly equivalent to East Asia. This scope would later include South Asia, centering on India, the Islamic sphere of West Asia, and Southeast Asia.

However, simply joining Eastern history to Western history will not make a history that applies to the entire world. The existing "world history" (i.e., Western history) has an academic system that was cultivated in the West, whereas Eastern history, which is based on classical Chinese archives, has a uniquely Chinese historical view and system of narrative. It is therefore impossible to mechanically combine Eastern history with Western history. Each must first be deconstructed, and then a history of the entire world must be built from scratch, using some new system.

It has taken much time to acknowledge the need for this work. The reason is that Western academia is content with the present Western history (i.e., what it deems "world history") and has advanced these ideas into world-systems theory and the global history doctrine. And even in studies in non-Western countries, practitioners on the whole merely follow these movements, compounding the historical mistakes of neglect and misunderstanding of Asia.

Conversely, it is no exaggeration to say that only in the domain of Eastern historical studies centered on Japan, which refused to be satisfied with the existing established world history, has a new world history system that includes Asia been continuously conceived.

This book is the latest effort in this regard. In it, I have attempted to combine academic tradition with the latest findings in the field, assemble and condense these into a concise new system, and express this new system with both general and academic audiences in mind.

It begins with a brief introduction to and critique of the history of the doctrine of "world history" up to global history, followed by a presentation of the Asian framework of "Asian history" that has formed the premodern mainstream in its place. From this base, the book traces Asian history from the birth of ancient civilizations to the rise and fall of the Mongol Empire. The demise of the latter in the fourteenth century provides an inflection point where the course of "Asian history" changes, entering a historical trajectory in which Europe secures hegemony. After outlining this historical process through the twentieth century, the book concludes by reexamining Japan's position in "Asian history" and world history.

Unfortunately, Eastern historical studies is truly a minority field in the larger domains of world and Japanese historical studies. Moreover, as the field has Japan at its center, the field labors under the linguistic handicap of being in Japanese, a language that is not in common usage around the world. Thus, this new world history system remains largely unknown in the wider world, the present book being no exception.

There has been no shortage of efforts to induce me to publish an English version of this book, on the premise that such language constraints are inconvenient in the present era of globalization. It is an unexpected pleasure to have been fortuitously afforded the opportunity to do so.

Non-Japanese readers of this book may feel uncomfortable. But it is my hope that they will realize the existence and significance of the activity, albeit but a fragment, that Japanese historical scholarship has engaged in over the past century and more, shedding Eurocentrism in an attempt to create a different picture of history from that of established "world history." I thank my readers in advance for pointing out any errors or omissions in the text.

The work of producing this translation began in 2021, and has reached publication in practically no time at all. This is due entirely to the efforts of Dr. Kobayashi Ryosuke, associate professor, Kyushu University, who reviewed the text during the translation process, ensuring accuracy in historical terminology; the translation and editorial team of Michael House, Koyanagi Takayuki, Eugene Tarshis, and Leslie Castro-Woodhouse; and Teshima Aki of the Japan Publishing Industry Foundation for Culture (JPIC). I take this space to express my thanks to you all.

Okamoto Takashi

A JAPANESE CONCEPTION OF WORLD HISTORY

What Constitutes World History for Most People

A long time ago, I read *A History of the World in 10 1/2 Chapters* by Julian Barnes. It was described as a novel, which to me means "fiction"—not something I'm in the habit of reading. Hence, I was likely drawn to it by the "History of the World" in the title. (Perhaps a little embarrassingly, it would seem that even my leisure reading must occasionally relate to my vocation of historian.)

It proved to be a rather entertaining read, with a plot structure that began with Noah's ark and continued through the Minoan civilization, the Wars of Religion, the voyages of Christopher Columbus, the wreck of the *Medusa*, the sinking of the *Titanic*, the Holocaust, the Jesuit missionaries, and the first moon landing.

On finishing this book, with its matter-of-fact sweep of history from the Bible and Western mythology to modern times, I realized something: the book's "history of the world" did not include Asia.

As this was a novel, however, and thus intended as entertainment, I thought there was no great cause for alarm. Before long, I had completely forgotten about it. Looking back, however, I see its publication might have been more significant than I'd originally thought, for the very reason that the novel had been in wide circulation: it represented conventional wisdom about what constituted the "history of the world."

The West: Universal and World History

Modern scholarship of all stripes has its origins in the West. From the outset, such endeavors have been inseparable from Christianity—particularly

Catholicism. It is easy to forget that among fields of modern scholarship, history has the closest ties with Christianity.

As the natural sciences derived from astrology and alchemy, so too is history indivisible from the Bible and Western mythology. The so-called "history of the world" ultimately derives from the "universal history" of Christianity. Seen through modern eyes, this story, proceeding from Adam and Eve and Noah's ark, is utterly preposterous as a historical narrative. As we have already seen, that story was not only an acceptable subject for a novel in a European language but calling it "A History of the World" seemed to suffice to make it acceptable as such.

However, I wonder how many Japanese are likely to associate world history with Christianity's universal history. I imagine the majority would incline toward recollections of their high school textbooks on world history. And even if not, I suspect that they would still be unlikely to associate history with the West or Christianity in particular.

The work of recording and describing the past existed in civilizations other than those in the West, irrespective of form, including Japan. Thus, people are inclined to assume without evidence that history is the same at all times and in all places. The theory of a "history of the world" may well be an archetype of this belief.

The academic field of historical studies emerged in the modern West, and accordingly adheres strictly to Western methodologies in its study and writing. Evidence for this exists beyond such obvious technical aspects as logic and proof. These methodologies are applied to the very assumptions underlying the field of historical studies. And since they underpin the field, these assumptions are all the more difficult to detect. Take, for example, even the most fundamental notions of time and space, which have been heavily influenced by Christianity.

Time in this context means the B.C.–A.D. chronology, with its accompanying concepts of progress and advancement. It is as natural as breathing for us to speak of "the year 2018" or to speak of "tomorrow" being "another day," showing how thoroughly we have internalized these Westernized concepts.

The era of Genesis in Christian doctrine corresponds to the aforementioned B.C.–A.D. chronology, and the "Last Judgment" to progress and advancement. And the fact remains that these concepts, whose absurd religiosity has faded through their eventual adaptation and secularization, arose out of the beliefs of Western peoples.

It once was second nature for East Asian peoples to use names for eras—"Qianlong" (1736–1795) in Chinese or "Heisei" (1989–2019) in Japanese, for example—and to speak of things being better in times past. Such conventions have long since fallen out of favor.

The same is true for ideas of space. The academic field of history came into existence in the nineteenth century, when the concept of the nation was established. And the concept of the nation was an invention of the Christian West. Historical studies accordingly began with the nation as subject and scope—in other words, "national history."

Because no Western nation exists in isolation, a larger stage was needed: the "world," as conceived by Westerners. The history of nations other than one's own thus came to be called "world history." We see this conception reflected in modern terminology as well, its range denoted by expressions like "family of nations" or its more modern equivalent, "international community."

When these terms first came into use, however, they were applied solely to the Christianized West. Furthermore, there was no palpable need to take into consideration any other framework for constructing national histories. The only world that those early scholars of history accepted was one of Christianity and nation.

Approaches toward a Global History

These were the premises of the study of history and of "world history." Up to now, there have been many "history of the world" narratives derived from this starting point, though these intrinsic premises remain unchanged. Certain constants persist in the conceptual framework that forms the foundation of their ideas and logic.

"World history" and the study of history are at heart a reflection of the Christian Bible's universal history. As the Enlightenment progressed, the historical narrative also became secularized, rationalized, and divorced from religion. Nonetheless, the progressive view of history and the spatial perception that only Christianity constituted the civilized world—both of which arose from the Christian worldview—remained stubbornly entangled with this conceptual framework.

The concept of *Geist* (mind/spirit) as conceived by Georg Wilhelm Friedrich Hegel (1770–1831) is representative of this Christian framework. Using the concept to draw a contrast to progressive Christian Europe, Hegel declared that China, India, and the rest of non-Christian Asia were completely stagnant, and lay outside of history.

A reformulation of these notions into materialist or economic terms yields Marxism, an entirely different construct within the same framework. Hegel's idea of stagnation has its equivalent in the Asiatic mode of production, which Karl Marx (1818–1883) placed beyond the scope of his notions of class struggle.

There was thus no acknowledgment of a world or a history outside of the West prior to Marxist history. From there, however, recognition at last began to dawn. For a post-materialist grand theory of world history, we have the world-systems theory promulgated by sociologist Immanuel Wallerstein (1930–2019). This idea hinges on framing the world in relation to the West. Whereas in premodern times there were world empires that coexisted both within and without the West, in modern times a world system has emerged with the developed West representing the core sector around which everything else is nothing more than a dependent peripheral.

While Wallerstein's recognition of a portion of the systematized world outside the West marks a significant change, the West nonetheless remains at its core, and that which is outside the West is excluded from the West's advances. In this sense, Wallerstein does not deviate from Christianity, Hegel, or Marx.

By contrast, sociologist Andre Gunder Frank (1929–2005) critiques this view. In his book *ReOrient*, Frank states that in premodern times, the non-Western world—China in particular—was the accumulator of wealth, which was in turn bestowed on the West. Due to his unfamiliarity with the Asian historical record, however, Frank makes no reference to the modes of progress and stagnation outside the West. Thus, his writing is simply the inverse of Wallerstein's.

Global history supersedes all of these approaches. It attempts to render world history in terms that have not traditionally been subjects for historical study, such as ecology. Moreover, the field of global history represents an effort to come to grips with subjects and issues common to the world at large.

In such aspects as perspective, concepts, or collection and usage of data, however, global history employs precisely the same standards and methodologies found in Western history. Hence, it merely enlarges on these same basic elements without examination, mediation, or critique. A prime example is the historical comparison of GDP by Angus Maddison (1926–2010) (Fig. 1), which is wholly untrustworthy owing to outrageously arbitrary estimates of the Eastern world prior to the eighteenth century.

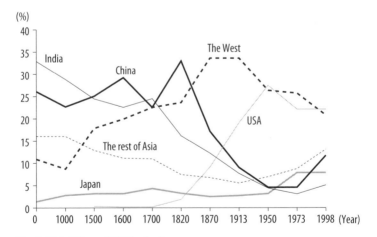

Fig. 1. Global Share of GDP by Region
A glance at the Ming and Qing dynasty periods is enough to show the arbitrariness of the graph. It estimates that per capita GDP "stagnated" for three hundred years after 1500, which is practically impossible.
Based on data from Angus Maddison, *The World Economy: A Millennial Perspective* (Paris: OECD Development Centre, 2001), 263, Appendix B, Table B-20: Shares of World GDP, 20 Countries and Regional Totals, 0–1998 A.D.

Eurocentrism

We refer to this phenomenon of the unexamined use of Western standards and methodologies as Eurocentrism, and there have long been calls to abandon it. I have heard that Wallerstein broke with it, as did Frank, and that even the idea of global history itself represents an escape from it. After some thirty years, however, Eurocentrism persists.

Then there is the California School, led by Kenneth L. Pomeranz (b. 1958), which represents the East Asian/economic history interpretation of global history. This school of thought paints the West and China as having undergone a great divergence in modern times, and presumes them to have been homogeneous prior to the eighteenth century.

The intent of the school's adherents was to reflect on Eurocentrism and attempt self-criticism of the idea of Eurocentric economic development. And the largest segment of participants in this discipline— namely, researchers in the Chinese-language region who traditionally have had a strong sense of inferiority vis-à-vis the West—praised it highly, making it a primary field of global research in no time. These researchers may have done so out of a sense of identification with the school's position.

There would be no problem if the assertions of the California School were true. At the very least, however, their statistical analyses and historical narratives with regard to East Asia are extremely careless, making a myriad of basic factual errors. One can only shake one's head in disbelief when informed, say, that seventeenth-century Japan was a place of profound political instability.

False premises and flawed methodologies lead to erroneous results. The notion of forcibly homogenizing East and West, for example, fits with Maddison's assumptions.

Treating East and West as homogeneous would seem to be tantamount to having done some soul-searching and reappraisal. At the root of this notion, however, is the idea that being the same as the West means not being inferior but superior. We find ourselves right back where we started: with Eurocentrism.

What all of these ideas have in common is that they fail both at attempting to inquire into the particulars of Asian history and at constructing logical arguments from such inquiries. Those failures give the impression that they need speak only of the West, and that Asia and indeed the rest of the world can be dismissed out of hand. But this will not do. Consider this excerpt from an essay by Kawakita Minoru (b. 1940), a Japanese authority on Western history:

> However, in the twenty-first century, East Asia is making great economic strides, whether one views the whole of the region or such individual nations as Taiwan, China, or South Korea. We can go further and assert that East Asia is undergoing rapid homogenization, or Westernization, and the Weberian approach is inadequate to explain the facts of the matter. . . . The present-day world is becoming increasingly intertwined, both economically and politically. The historical subject, therefore, should be not individual nations, but larger regions such as the West, East Asia, or the whole world. Such a view is gaining in popularity under such names as world-systems theory and global history. Whereas China and the West were both concerned with the limits of natural resources prior to industrialization, the Age of Discovery brought the West a windfall in the form of tremendous resource extraction from the Americas, which it leveraged to bring about the Industrial Revolution. This is the world-systems theory as promulgated by such American historians as Wallerstein and Pomeranz. This theory is far more persuasive when it comes to explaining such economic advancement as it continues into the present. (Kawakita, "Purotestantizumu dakara hatten?," 57)

In Kawakita's formulation, "making great economic strides" is thus made equivalent to homogeneity with the West. Does this mean, however, that there is homogeneity between the Japanese postwar growth period and economic advancement in China, to name just two examples? If so, that would mean ignoring the particulars of both cases.

The line of thought here advocates expanding "The historical subject [to] larger regions such as the West, East Asia, or the whole world," despite a failure to perceive or understand the history and factual circumstances of East Asia. This is an example of the idea that one can a priori treat historical conditions unique to the West—and concepts extracted therefrom—as universal and apply them to the world at large. This idea has existed since the concept of universal history was invented.

And this is by no means the fault of just one historian. I would venture to say that the majority of learned persons act this way. It shows just how entrenched are the reliance on, the deference to, and indeed the faith in the doctrines and mindsets of Westerners.

National History, Japanese History, and Eastern History

The narrative unit of history since the commencement of historical studies has typically been the nation. Criticisms exposing the harms of such "national histories" began long ago. Nonetheless, it is true that history itself describes the process of the rise of nation-states, and that we are even now living in these nation-states. We cannot fully extricate ourselves from "national histories," however we might find fault with, criticize, or deny them.

According to the Western mode of thought, national histories are self-evidently connected with European history. The history of the West, whether political or economic, consists wholly of aspects that transcend the bases of individual countries. What is national thus necessarily becomes international. And this international European/Western history quite naturally expands to become the history of the world. It was European imperialism that came to dominate the world, after all.

This is the structure of Western historical sensibilities. And there is no feeling whatsoever of these sensibilities being out of place, so long as the matter is confined to Western history. Such sensibilities lie at the root of all the grand theories which have until now been intimately bound up with world history.

Conversely, non-Western people who find these sensibilities to be alien will never fully identify with them, because such people have no sense of their authenticity.

Let us apply the formula to Japan, for example. As with Western history, Japanese history is systematized into ancient, medieval, and early modern, with regard to both periodization and stages of advancement.

So far, all is well. But as a national history, Japanese history does not connect particularly well with the history of East Asia. While there are direct links between Japanese and Western history in early modern and modern terms, that is about as far it goes.

Many scholars of Japanese history researching East Asian history prior to the modern period, whether working before or after World War II, all but ignored the findings of Eastern historians. And from the perspective of specialists in Eastern historical studies, even when such scholars wrote of Japanese history in ways that encompassed East Asian history, they misplaced their emphases in their historical narratives, resulting in gross errors and distortions in the worst cases. It is inexcusable that such a state of affairs is allowed to persist. Only in recent times has academia, at last, begun to show some belated self-awareness of this situation.

The first thing that comes to mind when one mentions foreign or world history to a Japanese person is Western history. Who cares whether Eastern/Asian history is ignored or misunderstood? It is this all-too-typical sensibility on the part of Japanese that strikes me as the most critical problem of all.

East and West

The field of Eastern historical studies has not succeeded in establishing the kind of periodization structure that is taken for granted in Western or Japanese history. The old ways of expressing periods with names of rulers or dynasties, such as the Han (206 B.C.–220 A.D.) or the Tang (618–907), remain unchallenged to this day.

Research into these periods, however, has brought much evidence to light. It is now clear that not all of this history can be pigeonholed into concepts derived from Western history such as feudalism or capitalism.

These developments signify that there are instances in which Western historical methodologies may be insufficient to explain the East Asian historical record. In other words, we have learned intimately from Eastern historical studies that there can be no fundamental law or standard model for world history.

Accordingly, this field has instead sought to deepen individual research topics in line with primary sources. This effort has coincided with dramatic improvements in printing and information technologies beginning in the 1990s. Research since then has made great strides and been quite fruitful.

With the loss of any grand theory, however, comes a situation in which it seems the richer we are in new historical evidence, the more complicated the overall systemization becomes, making it that much more difficult to return to a history of the world. The field of Eastern historical studies has been precariously close to disappearing, left as a mere coexistence of separate, fragmented studies.

In this situation, global history bears down on us from the West. Remarkable progress has been made in research into Western as well as Eastern history, thanks to technological innovations. In conjunction with the trend toward globalization, there is a steady inclination toward formulating a history of the entire world. And it is only natural that Eastern historical studies and Asian historical research should fall within its scope.

Both prior Western history and more recent global history have neglected almost the entirety of Asian history's concrete facts as well as the fertile researches into them. Even as Asian history has been ignored, however, there has been magnanimity in recognizing such ignorance, with the recognition itself deemed worthy of respect. The present situation, though, is akin to running wild, with globalization as a pretext.

There is a strong inclination among Japanese in recent times to casually assume that they understand those historical circumstances, particularly with regard to East Asia. It is natural that Western global history would struggle with Asian historical studies written in Japanese or Chinese, as Chinese and other Asian languages and cultures are challenging in the extreme for Westerners to comprehend. Conversely, Japanese specialists have extensive research findings in Asian history studies in their native language. And yet, it never ceases to perplex me how it is that, without having read these native-language writings on the subject, these same Japanese specialists think nothing of discussing global history "from the Asian viewpoint."

Take Japanese research into the history of the British Empire, for example. When commenting on the place of China in this history, scholars rely on and liberally cite research papers and other texts in English and other Western languages. Why is it that Japanese scholars such as Akita Shigeru (b. 1958) and Haneda Masashi (b. 1953), who provide impetus for global history in Japanese historical scholarship, turn to such superficial Western publications rather than the research findings of Japanese scholars writing in Japanese?

The East-West Differential

Perhaps it boils down to a belief by Japanese specialists in Western studies that Western ideas are more easily understood—even given the language barrier—than Eastern studies originating in Japan. A considerable gap would then exist between East and West.

A bare-bones summary of the situation of Western history in global history might be as follows: as a rule, Western history has exhaustively elucidated all civic aspects—chiefly politics, diplomacy, societies, and cultures—of its own "world." The attention of the field has necessarily expanded outward from this "world" as result, in a manner similar to the imperialist expansion of the British Empire.

In tandem with this global expansion, Western history has moved away from a focus on the politics, diplomacy, and culture of the histories of individual Western nations, which are necessarily demarcated by national borders and in which real people are visible, and toward such themes as economics and the environment, which are faceless and easily transcend national borders. Accordingly, fields such as quantitative economics, ecology, and disease therapies have thus become the key thesis subjects and points of contention in depicting so-called world history.

Nor can we overlook the fact that English has become the lingua franca of globalization. The English language and Western numerical indices have been organized into supranational modes which anyone can understand, facilitating a global historical narrative.

Put another way, global history only makes sense in the light of such themes and modes. Areas like politics and diplomacy are already stale, and excluded from the outset. This is acceptable so long as matters are confined to Western history, where the broad outlines of politics and societies have long since been clarified and consensus has been reached. Therefore, it has been possible to engage freely with areas of history like ecology and quantitative economics, where the human element is less tangible.

The same cannot be said of all possible worlds, however. The field of Eastern historical studies is still at a far less mature stage than that of Western history, which flatters itself as having learned all there is to know about society. Eastern historical studies has not fully illuminated the shape and substance of politics and diplomacy, let alone social structures. Periodization itself is not possible, even in Chinese history, whose source materials are arguably the most extensive and well analyzed of any history.

Having long clung to the time-honored techniques and findings of Western history, Eastern historical studies is now in the midst of a reconstruction through newly uncovered primary sources. The shape of Asian history may or may not be illuminated via the same standards and methodologies by which research into Western history arrived at global history. The outcome is still unknown as of this writing.

History as Seen from an Asian Standpoint

Such are the differences that exist in the progress and standards of research between East and West, Asia and Europe. Accordingly, orientations and methodologies also vary between them. This is the prime reason that Western researchers fail to understand Eastern history. The lion's share of responsibility can of course be attributed to a lack of dedication on their part. Yet there is also a degree of doubt regarding claims that there has been sufficient investigation and communication for the East to be understood by outsiders.

In any case, there is a vast gap between Eastern or Asian history and Western history. And it would be inappropriately hasty, even premature, to apply global history as is to the former in spite of this.

Since Wallerstein and Frank, Western history has long acknowledged the existence of historical developments other than those of the West. The perspective of modernization has shifted from a unitary, unilinear Western model to one premised on pluralism and multilinearity. Nonetheless, the same global history that is applied to Western history has been applied to the non-European world—and to Asia in particular—by Pomeranz, for example.

The fact remains that scholars, carried away by the preconception of "history of the world," have forcibly placed the East on a par with the West. They insist on making the means of analysis used in both instances the same: "homogeneous," whether it be language, concepts, indices, or statistics. In so doing, they demonstrate a disregard for the particular historical facts at issue. It should come as no surprise that a large quantity of errors has arisen as a consequence.

What appears to be operative here is an idée fixe in which theories and indices abstracted via Western methodologies are applied a priori. Whether the materialistic conception of history or statistical values, each is nothing more than a theory or an index abstracted from actual facts. A sort of precondition is in force: for subjects and concerns that meet the condition, a concise, clear answer may be obtained; but for others, no purpose is served.

Japanese studies of Eastern history long ago put forth the idea that it ought to be possible to resolve the facts about the East with the theories and indices of the West. Attempts to bring the idea to fruition, however, came to a pathetic end. And the present idea of global history recapitulates the old idea of a fundamental law for world history, as unre-constructed as ever.

And yet, it is only just and proper that Japanese research into world history, possessed of its own Eastern historical studies—for which understanding of the neighboring East Asian region is critical—should distinctly differ from this approach. It should be possible for—nay, it is incumbent upon—such Japanese research into world history to reveal the historical particulars of Asia, which have thus far been neglected by Westerners and Chinese alike, and to assemble the form of that history.

World History as Understood by the Japanese

World history, which ultimately arrives at global history—especially its theorizing and abstraction—is founded on the premise that societies are homogeneous the world over. Fallacies lurk in that premise and process.

There are many historical facts and sources in Asia that are difficult to perceive and comprehend from the conventional European standpoint. Therefore, conceiving a world history in unity with Asia would require us to question the accepted wisdom of Western historical studies, and to reconsider history's very premises from the logic and perspective of Asian history itself.

That charge is best suited to the Japanese, who possess Eastern histor-ical studies and need to know East Asian history. We have the resources, are blessed with the ability, and also have abundant need.

However, the Japanese, and in particular Japanese intellectuals, hav-ing assimilated Western studies, have by no means read Eastern histor-ical studies written in Japanese, nor do they have any respect for their findings. In prior times, it might have been sufficient for only experts in the field to consider such matters. In the present age of globalization, however, a mutual East-West awareness is more essential than ever.

While the age of globalization has brought about an integrated, border-less planet, it has also rendered an even greater localism, or more emphat-ically, self-righteousness, as exemplified by such phenomena as terrorism. A deluge of information has made it impossible to exercise discrimination in judging good or bad, right or wrong. This has created a social climate in which superficial knowledge is allowed to spread, where people see only what they want to see and hear only what they want to hear.

In historical terms, there is a prevailing ideological/political view of history that ignores sources and data, as in the "historical perceptions" that China professes. One could even go so far, however, as to say that there does not seem to be much that distinguishes this from the "clash of civilizations" or "global history." Sinocentric remarks have something in common with Eurocentrism in terms of perspective, conception, and sensibility.

How, then, should Japanese (this author included) respond, caught as we are between these two poles? If we Japanese are to avoid the aforementioned pitfall of self-righteousness, our only choice is to write a history following the just path of historical studies, to correct our biased perceptions with a wider field of view and rectify our distorted history. Hence there is a need for a narrative of world history based on authentic Asian historicity.

CHAPTER 1

ASIAN HISTORY AND ANCIENT CIVILIZATIONS

1. Asian History: Conception and Configuration

The Present State of Eastern Historical Studies

However I may strive to write a history of the world, I am but one Japanese scholar specializing in Eastern history. As this is an inadequate position for discourse, I must begin by at least recognizing and keeping in mind the strengths and weaknesses of academic tradition as well as the limits and shortcomings in my own knowledge and ability.

Eastern history is one branch of history. It does not consist of any particularly unusual methodologies. It started by drawing on the origins of history and the preconceptions and analytical devices of Western history.

One such device is the aforementioned application of periodization structures. There is no other way to model Western concepts or the progress of Western history. Miyazaki Ichisada (1901–1995), a leading light of Eastern historical studies, exemplified this position. Miyazaki's mentor, historian Naito Konan (1866–1934), propounded a periodization of Chinese history in which he placed the early modern period in the Northern Song dynasty period (960–1127). Miyazaki updated and strengthened the argument of Naito's theory, ascertaining and describing the early modern times that the theory encompassed by means of such concepts as nationalism and capitalism. Nor did Miyazaki restrict himself to these early modern times. He further asserted that the theory of the polis or city-state applied to ancient Chinese times and that medieval Chinese aristocracy should have been described in terms of feudalism. By citing such Western concepts, Miyazaki was far more thorough in this regard than Naito, who was indifferent to modern Western civilization.

Even now, I find Miyazaki's works highly readable and easy to understand. I can scarcely believe that they were written by someone born more than a hundred years ago. The reason his points are always clear, aside from the quality of his writing, lies in his logic, reasoning, and handling of concepts. As Western concepts occupy the greater part of our minds—our knowledge—Miyazaki has many supporters and detractors alike.

The present-day field of Eastern historical studies at the very least, however, is no longer amenable to such narratives. There is far more skepticism about Western concepts than there used to be. Such skepticism begins with discovering new primary sources and continues with making detailed elucidations and positioning of historical evidence.

The Eastern Historical Studies Bottleneck

People versed only in Western concepts, however, are by no means assured of grasping such historical facts. They do not understand the labels and concepts involved.

When referring to a city-state, whereas Miyazaki spoke of "polis," in the Greco-Roman sense of the word, the term *yusei kokka* has largely taken its place among Japanese historians, in accordance with original Chinese terminology. What used to be a "guild" is now *hanghui* in Chinese. Words such as *denko* in Japanese or *dianhu* in Chinese (possibly equivalent to "peasant," "tenant farmer," or "serf" in English, depending on context), which have been points of contention in periodization debates, have been used as is from the outset of such studies and for all intents and purposes are untranslatable.

It is likely more accurate to use these original expressions as they occur in primary sources. However, it is incumbent on one to study Chinese history to a fair degree of expertise in order to comprehend the meanings of the words. How different such expressions are from capitalism, nationalism, and other commonly used Western concepts.

A structure has thus emerged that does not allow easy admittance to novices or laypersons. Take, for example, *waqf* (possibly equivalent to "endowment" or "donation" in English) in Islamic countries, or *zamindar* (possibly equivalent to "landowner" or "seigneur" in English) in India.

It is due to such contexts as this, where what is true of the smallest part is similarly true of the whole, that those affiliated with other disciplines—including but not limited to Western history—find the content of Asian history to be increasingly forbidding and incomprehensible. Eventually, without the help of Western concepts, such scholars lose any interest in the very subject of Eastern historical studies.

Therefore, it was incumbent first and foremost on researchers in the field of Eastern historical studies, being the responsible parties that knew how matters stood, to acknowledge the problem and then do something about it. The upper echelons of academia, however, have failed to fulfill these responsibilities to any satisfactory degree. This is due to having their hands full of new materials and doctrines, and to a desire to avoid premature theorizing and error. The problems and significance of the old debates over periodization structures are also now forgotten within the scope of Eastern historical studies, precluding their being communicated elsewhere.

A Fresh Look at Periodization

Japanese Eastern historical studies has seen a number of research frameworks and conceptions relating to world history. One such conception is periodization.

We need not resort to the "Great Divergence" described by Pomeranz to observe the historical phenomenon that Asia and Europe had been growing apart beginning in the nineteenth century. This circumstance used to be called modernization. The very idea of periodization resides in an awareness of the problem of how to understand the course of events leading up to this so-called divergent modern period.

Such an awareness was common across historical studies in general. And that common understanding made such expressions as "fundamental law of world history" tenable in the first place. Periodization should instead be seen as a comparison and comprehension of East and West in chronological terms.

The task then necessarily becomes one of ascertaining where and how chronological progress differs between East and West, with the modern period as a foundation. And such a comparison must assume homogeneous elements. Eastern historical studies hit a wall when it was discovered that elements that were assumed to be homogeneous were in fact heterogeneous.

One approach is to look at the situation with fresh eyes. Having already touched on the particulars of periodization debates in Eastern historical studies, I will not rehash the subject here. It is important to keep in mind, however, that awareness of the spatial scope in question is minimal on the part of both Eastern and Western historical scholarship, and apt to be taken as a given, as being self-evident.

Taking "West" to mean only "the West" and "East" to mean only "East Asia," and thus to reflexively exclude Central Asia when speaking of "Asia," shows a propensity toward self-satisfaction on the part of the Japanese. What Japanese mean by "East Asia" is only the Japanese archipelago together with those areas with which the archipelago is immediately concerned, namely, the Korean Peninsula and mainland China. It is perhaps the counterpart of that dyed-in-the-wool Eurocentric belief that outside of the West, there is only Japan.

A Fresh Look at the History of East-West Interactions

Along these lines, I propose to focus on the lineage of the history of East-West interactions. This area of research is exemplified by the technical concept known as the Silk Road and has continued unbroken therefrom.

While drawing on Sinology since the Edo period (1603–1867), Japanese Eastern historical studies, which began in the Meiji period (1868–1912), shows a marked tendency to avoid mention of China itself. This tendency was a reaction to China's own Sinocentrism at the time, which in turn was a reaction to the rising tide of Japan's own nationalism. That is why scholars of the time directed considerable research effort in particular to regions referred to by such *kango* (Sino-Japanese terminology) as *saigai* (north of the Great Wall) or *seiiki* (Western Regions). Copious research has been gathered since then. Such research began with inquiries into the historical evidence of place names expressed in Chinese characters and extended into the subjects of cultural exchange, religion, civics, politics, military matters, and ecology.

In earlier times, as indicated by the name of Silk Road, these regions were considered only as being along a road connecting East and West. As silk formerly could only be obtained from China, Silk Road became another name for China and connoted a road by which silk was conveyed to the West— namely, to Europe.

Nowadays, however, advances in research have led to an understanding that the road itself was a historical staging ground of prime importance. The technical concept of the Central Eurasian world represents this very conversion in our perspective.

One might call this a comprehension of East and West seen anew in spatial terms. Originally, as may be inferred from the very label "East-West interactions," the East and the West in question were practically obvious. Nowadays, however, this notion has shifted significantly, as can also be inferred from how the concept is expressed. The "central" region, which was once only a road for relations between Western Europe and East Asia, is now treated as Eurasia, combining both East and West.

Conversely, the chronological progress of Central Eurasian history remains opaque, as it did when the region was referred to as the Silk Road. Granted, much historical evidence has come to light, and changes abound. However, the thread of these changes has yet to firmly anchor itself in our minds.

One reason is that minds conditioned to accept the notion of Western modernity have difficulty grasping such changes. This difficulty arises from a lack of elements that connect these changes to the stages of progress and modernization that have become indices of East-West periodization. While if anything this problem is on the part of the observer, our minds are nonetheless not going to be changed on the spot, with no questions asked.

Thus, we see that there are inadequacies on all fronts. One solution would be to look at the situation from the opposite point of view. It should be possible to devise a new conception of world history by reevaluating periodization and advances in the history of East-West relations in combination with a new view of chronology and regional space.

Pioneering Conceptions

In this regard, Japanese historians have made various efforts, some of which have been pioneering. We need only cite the Asian history of Miyazaki Ichisada and the ecological view of history promoted by ecologist and cultural anthropologist Umesao Tadao (1920–2010) as primary examples. Both of these theories are high-order abstractions combining periodization and regional demarcation. A comparison of these alone will suffice to reveal the distinctive features of these modes of thought, and make their respective strengths and weaknesses clear.

Miyazaki draws on a timeline with Europe as its reference to express his idea of world history (see Fig. 2). This would seem a conventional methodology, given that it was conceived from the periodization used in Eastern historical studies. What makes it original, however, is that it divides East Asia and West Asia into relatively independent regions, combines them with Europe, and incorporates the relations among these three regions and the dynamism of the impact that they have on one another.

Umesao, on the other hand, conceived of regions as ecologies anchoring clusters of people. The expression of this idea was necessarily as a map (Fig. 4, p. 39), and the idea represents a significant contribution as it renders the regional structure of Eurasia comprehensible at a glance.

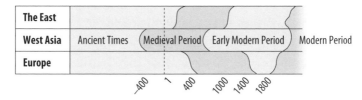

Fig. 2. Condensed Timeline of World History
Reproduced from Miyazaki Ichisada, *Chugoku shi* [History of China] (Tokyo: Iwanami Shoten, 2015), 23.

While this graphical depiction alone is insufficient to make changes over time clearly understood, Umesao takes up the question of feudalism in the body of his text, showing that the viewpoint is not lacking. In fact, this conception has led to numerous revisions and updates, including a maritime view of history and civilization. As an example, economist Kawakatsu Heita (b. 1948) has pointed out that Umesao's model takes only a land-based view, and he has proposed an alternate model that also includes a maritime-based view (Kawakatsu, *Bunmei no kaiyo shikan* [A Maritime Historical View of Civilization]).

Both of these theories date back more than sixty years. However, newer is not necessarily better for historical research, unlike in the natural sciences. Later generations may be said to have an obligation to promote the forgotten achievements of their predecessors.

These conceptions were assembled in completely different disciplines along disparate vectors. And yet, it happens that they stand in a complementary relationship to one another and have much in common. This will help lead us forward.

Where to Start

The first thing that these theories have in common is the seemingly trivial point that East Asia does not consist solely of the Japanese archipelago, the Korean Peninsula, and mainland China. However apparent that geography may seem, its obviousness makes it more likely to be overlooked. Among many intellectuals in Japan and elsewhere, there is a lack of perspectives that take the rest of Asia, as well as the West, as scope for research, denote each of these relative to the others, and interrelate them all.

This is, in fact, what comes of neither knowing nor wanting to know about Asia. Past Japanese reverence for Eastern and Chinese historical studies, for example, had motives other than learning about Asia in itself. Such reverence was, rather, simply a shadow cast by the fashionable thought of the time, whether it was prewar Japan's imperialism or the Communism of the postwar period. The other side of that coin can be seen in present-day Japanese turning exclusively to the West, driven by globalization, and instead neglecting Eastern and Chinese historical studies.

Dispelling such conventional wisdom requires formulating a point of view positing that in reality there are many Asias, and considering these many Asias in combination. Both Miyazaki's and Umesao's theories offer this perspective.

The Miyazaki timeline shown in Figure 2 depicts only East Asia and West Asia, and thus can perhaps be seen as differing from Umesao's theory, which includes South Asia in its scope. However, Miyazaki has another line of inquiry, in which he delineates regional demarcations according to arrangement of characters in varying writing systems (see Fig. 5, p. 42), which harmonizes perfectly with Umesao's ecological demarcations (Fig. 4). As I will elaborate in the next section, it is possible not only to conceive of coherent regions comprising the entities of East, West, and South Asia but also to perceive them as having common structures yet drastically different cultures.

The second commonality of these theories is that they both assign unique positions to Japan and the West. While the former is not represented in the Miyazaki timeline, Miyazaki's other inquiry argues for Japan being an underdeveloped hinterland vis-à-vis Asia, as can be easily seen in the timeline in Figure 3. His theory also corresponds in this way with that of Umesao, in which Japan is considered its own world. That

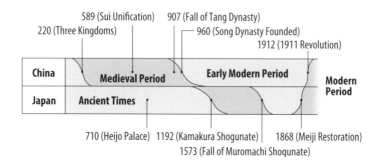

Fig. 3. Comparison of Japanese and Chinese Periods
Adapted from Miyazaki Ichisada, *Chugoku shi* [History of China] (Tokyo: Iwanami Shoten, 2015), 28.

Miyazaki accords a position of peculiarly special status to Europe, the yardstick of his timeline, does not contradict Umesao's theory, which also puts Western Europe and Japan in their own worlds.

The regional structure that emerges from this discussion, and that provides the stage for world history, facilitates consideration based first of all on the ecological view of history as propounded by Umesao (see Fig. 4). I propose to begin my inquiry here.

Regions within Asia

Eurasia is a gigantic landmass, with a comparatively short coastline yet a vast expanse of interior regions. Nor is it all one big flat grassland. In addition to almost impassable mountains and valleys, there are also desolate, barren deserts. In terms of living environments for clusters of people, these places form their own boundaries, dividing the land into a number of coherent areas. These are represented in Umesao Tadao's map (Fig. 4) as follows: I, East Asia; II, South Asia; and IV, West Asia.

In the center of the map are the Pamirs. The solid lines intersecting therein are mountain ranges forming the boundaries that divide the Eurasian interior. The littoral regions, subject to the monsoons, have a humid climate. The inland regions, far from the coasts, consequently have an arid climate. This distinction is also rendered in the figure by shading and additional lines. In other words, each of the map areas (I, II, and IV) corresponding to East, South, and West Asia, respectively, has a structure where regions of humid climate coexist to varying degrees with regions of arid climate.

Ecologies naturally differ as climates vary according to physical geography, as do ways of life relying for survival on those ecologies. Accordingly, anthropogeographic modes of economics, culture, and politics also differ among these ecologies.

Humid regions are conducive to a more settled lifestyle, in which grain is produced and survival effected through farming. This contrasts with the nomadic lifestyle of arid regions, where peoples are constantly on the move in search of grasslands to derive sustenance from herding livestock.

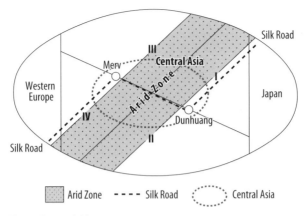

Fig. 4. Umesao's Map
Adapted from Umesao Tadao, *Bunmei no seitai shikan* [*An Ecological View of History*] (Tokyo: Chuokoronsha, 1974), 213.

East, South, and West Asia each evolved into overlapping, composite worlds of nomadism and farming, with various periods of conflict and coexistence. The outward protrusions of the West and Japan at the respective ends of the map are not merely a consequence of their being geographically located at the eastern and western ends of the continent. These protrusions also signify that these are foreign lands, outside the bounds of such composite worlds as areas I, II, and IV.

Thus, the history of the periods of conflict and coexistence in the overlapping worlds of areas I, II, and IV of Eurasia may be designated Asian history, exclusive of Europe. And it is these periods of conflict and coexistence that formed the fundamental pattern and the driving force of Asian history, which were absent from both Japanese and Western histories.

What Is the Silk Road?

Did regions I, II, and IV exist in isolation from one another? Probably not. It is unlikely that any single bond yoked East, South, and West Asia. However, if one were asked what the greatest connection among them was, the answer would almost certainly be the so-called Silk Road.

The question of why this artery of communication and commerce came into existence and persisted in that place and in that form is, of course, open to many interpretations; there is no single answer. One interpretation suggests itself, however, based on the above.

Every world history text includes a diagram of the Silk Road. However, such figures are insufficient to communicate why the Silk Road followed its particular route.

The Silk Road traverses Eurasia, running along a boundary line between nomads to the north and farmers to the south. On the preceding map (Fig. 4), this is indicated as a bold dashed line. The periphery of the dashed line transecting the arid zone on the map—the range along that line—is colloquially known as Central Asia. Oasis cities are strung along it from Dunhuang in the east to Merv in the west, across the Amu River.

As nomadism and farming are completely different lifestyles, their products and daily necessities also vary. Each can readily supply what the other lacks, making life better for both. Opportunities for trade and

Photo from History/David Henley/Bridgeman Images

barter thus arise on the boundary between nomads and farmers. Commerce emerges and grows out of these opportunities.

The Silk Road can be seen as coming into existence in this way: markets are built near the oasis cities in various areas; as they increase in density, they individually become strung together, ultimately becoming an artery for communication. Hence, it would be more appropriate to view the road as forming an east-west chain for north-south trade, rather than as a road distantly connecting East and West.

Nomadism, farming, and commerce: the history of Asia begins at the point where these elements come together.

2. Ancient Civilizations: The Start of Asian History

The Beginnings of Civilization

Having demarcated and configured the regions in question, we can now begin the narrative of Asian history.

A conventional start would likely be with the dawn of civilization. When my generation of Japanese was in high school, in the early 1980s, civilizations in this period were commonly referred to in world history classes as the *yondai bunmei*, or "four great ancient civilizations." From the outset, this framework contained a strong mixture of liberal helpings of Eurocentrism and imperialism. These preconceptions have begun to give way as a result of recent advances in paleography and archaeology. There are many points about these preconceptions where one must exercise restraint in judgment. The "four great ancient civilizations" label is being increasingly omitted from world history texts as well.

If one were to ask, however, whether there was a substitute conceptual framework, then the answer would probably be not yet. There is no significant difference between replacing the aforementioned "four great ancient civilizations" label in textbooks with an enumeration of the civilizations in question as the ancient Near East, the Indus, and the Huang

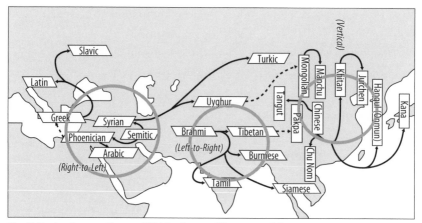

Fig. 5. Region Demarcations and Writing System Alignments of Characters

Reproduced from Miyazaki Ichisada, *Tozai kosho shiron* [Essays on the History of East-West Interaction], ed. Tonami Mamoru (Tokyo: Chuokoronsha, 1998), 58–59.

He (Yellow River). I will leave the minutiae to expert researchers. Instead, I propose to take up the broad canvas of developments, assembling only those issues meriting serious consideration, to present the narrative in question.

Writing systems are essential, regardless of whether one speaks of civilization, culture, or history. Hence, the phrase "ancient civilizations" indicates those first worlds of humankind to devise written language, leave records, and have a traceable history. What we have learned from the manner of these writing systems is that the positioning of ancient civilizations aligns with the gist of what has been presented in the preceding section regarding this subject.

The manner of a writing system refers to its alignment of characters. Whether to write vertically, from top to bottom, or horizontally, either left to right or right to left, is merely the simplest of differences. In a chapter from his work *Tozai kosho shiron* (Essays on the History of East-West Interaction), titled *"Rekishiteki chiiki to moji no hairetsu-ho"* (Historical Regions and Character Alignments in Writing Systems), Miyazaki writes as follows:

At heart, the direction in which a script is written is irrelevant, whether right to left, left to right, or top to bottom. . . . It is this very irrelevance, amidst the undeniable fact that a particular direction is established . . . that imparts sufficient force to tradition.

The very problem of a writing system's alignment of characters only arises in worlds that possess writing systems in the first place. And handing down writing systems to successive generations by building a framework of "tradition" around them has been necessary to their very existence since time immemorial.

The region we refer to as the ancient Near East, which ultimately settled on right-to-left writing, is within area IV, West Asia, in Figure 4. The Indus civilization, with left-to-right writing, is in area II, South Asia. And the Huang He civilization, with top-to-bottom writing, is in area I, East Asia. Even as far back as the dawn of civilization, there has been a correspondence between writing directions and ecological region demarcations.

How Nomadism Figures in the Scheme of Things

The first question that comes to mind concerns the origin of these ancient civilizations—although, of course, there is ultimately no way of identifying these for certain.

However, we do know that the cradles of ancient civilizations are found in places that are near great rivers, and thus amply supplied with water, while being nearly surrounded by arid zones and thus in proximity to nomads. This is true for the ancient Near East, the Indus of South Asia, and the Huang He of East Asia. It appears that desirable locations for the ancient civilizations are to be found in such places.

That being the case, we cannot give short shrift to the presence of these nomadic peoples. These very civilizations, capable of farming, accumulating wealth, and leaving remains in temperate places where water is plentiful, were built by settled farming peoples. But when the presence and the activities of the nomads, full of vitality in their movements, came near these places, these agriculturist peoples had no choice but to make contact and enter into exchange with them.

In such situations, it was necessary to have a means of recording and preserving a shared understanding in the course of forming and managing groups and organizations according to circumstances prone to change. Necessity being the mother of invention, it seems likely that writing scripts were thus created and propagated beginning in these times.

Suppose that the only occupations were nomadism or farming, and moreover, that there were no relations between them. In that case, even if organizations were to be created, it would suffice for each to observe and hand down the same lifestyle patterns among its own people from generation to generation. As this could be adequately achieved through word-of-mouth and custom, there was likely no need for written records. Prehistoric nomads had no writing systems, and there were more than a few agricultural civilizations that also lacked writing.

The second thing that comes to mind is how extensive was the growth of these civilizations, which would require military force that could cover a wide area. The presence of the nomads matters in this regard as well.

In the first place, nomadism is a way of life involving the search for grasslands suited to raising livestock. The chief activity of nomadic peoples is moving numerous times a year in a nearly periodic fashion between winter and summer quarters. The former, in which nomads pass the long harsh inland winters, are particularly crucial. Nomads who shared these places formed groups known as tribes or clans.

Horseback riding caught on in Central Asia some three thousand years ago. It was a truly great innovation, one that conferred previously unknown speed of movement, even as it involved such complex skills as the training and command of horses. Adapted to warfare, it also represented a kind of revolution in armaments, in that it dramatically increased mobility and enabled the annihilation of enemies by encirclement. This development changed the course of history then and thereafter.

Once such equestrian skills became commonplace, nomadic bands were immediately able to adapt their daily lives to military campaigns.

There came to be no distinction between nomad and soldier, which indicates how hard their lives were in ordinary terms. But in extraordinary times, in times of war, these peacetime survival bands promptly transformed into cavalry units.

This was utterly unlike settled agricultural peoples, who could not go far from their land and who treated peacetime and war as completely different conditions.

These peoples, with their large populations, assembled armed forces having superiority in numbers, material resources, and structures. Such advantages would likely have enabled them to surpass the aforementioned cavalry in individual battles and maneuvers. They were, however, entirely inferior in the most important aspect of warfare: mobility. Nor could they sustain a wartime footing for very long.

Thus, on the whole, the supremacy of cavalry and nomadism went unchallenged. Only nature, in the form of climate and geography, hindered nomads on horseback. No military force on earth could surpass them, and efforts to alter the situation long proved fruitless. The change would not happen until the gunpowder revolution of the sixteenth century, encompassing the invention of firearms and the discovery and harnessing of energy.

The Composition of Civilization

Umesao Tadao refers to arid zones, grassland regions, and nomads as "the source of great evil and destruction," "the seed of destruction," and "intense violence," thereby emphasizing their aggressive, destructive aspects (Umesao, *Bunmei no seitai shikan*, translated by Beth Carey as *An Ecological View of History: Japanese Civilization in the World Context*). The meaning is clear: more than anything else, the nomads excelled at force of arms. This was their military superiority.

That alone, however, will not suffice. Such rhetoric is spoken persistently from the standpoint of the settled farming peoples. In their position, these peoples would have been on the receiving end of seasonal, intermittent raiding and plunder. Thus, it stands to reason that their records would be a litany of such woes. But there is room to consider whether this was, in fact, the usual state of affairs.

The news exists to inform people of unusual situations, whether incidents or accidents. Reports of this kind are what frequently come down to us in the historical record. Were the facts—the everyday reality—to consist solely of news stories, society would be a terrible place to live in, as there would be nothing but traffic accidents and murders.

Daily business being conventional by nature, records were not kept of every customary act, accepted practice, or commonplace happening. The fact of these matters being taken for granted makes it that much harder to keep track of them in historical archives.

Therefore, nomads embarking on acts of aggression and/or destruction would be unusual, and not doing so would be normal. What, then, were their peacetime relations like? This is the matter that must be interrogated.

Like others, nomads needed daily necessities of life as well as luxuries. Some of these likely could be obtained only from the agricultural world. And there surely had to be a means of obtaining these things other than by raiding or robbery. There would be costs to doing so against ready and willing opponents, thus incurring risk to the nomads. Hence, armed aggression could not be the only choice open to the nomads; it would have been a last resort. There must have been less costly methods available to them.

Barter was possible: The nomads had horses, animal pelts, and dairy products, which the farming lands lacked, thereby facilitating trade. The farmers, excelling in crop yield, were in an even stronger position. A place emerged therein for merchants and commerce.

In all times and places, however, trade—which involves the exchange and delivery of property—brings with it hazards of one degree or another. Such problems, which are prone to occurring frequently, can range from discrepancies in setting prices and defaulting on one's debts to fraud and breach of trust.

The resource-poor nomads were particularly eager for trade and dependent on merchants. Even so, this was by no means a unilateral dependency. Merchants relied on the protection of the nomads to reduce the risks and hazards of trade. It was absolutely necessary to have superior military might on hand to prevent conflict and enforce penalties for violations. In this manner, both parties were easily united in a complementary relationship.

This construction is seen in history thereafter, for instance, in the trading caravans of the Silk Road. The caravans, together with the nomads, were frequently on the move. There were large trading partners near settled farming lands, and regular markets were established that could grow into even larger settlements. Examples of the latter were oasis cities, which formed political organizations when they grew larger still.

The Ancient Near East

Civilizations began where nomadism, commerce, and agriculture thus intersected. It was true of all the ancient civilizations, in terms of location conditions.

The oldest of these is the ancient Near East. It has been said that civilization is writing, and these ancient states required written communication and records, as well as organizations based on them. These ancient states also left remains, archives, and other artifacts that have survived to the present day. And they engaged with neighboring tribes and nearby nomads. The vicissitudes of the states of the ancient Near East are likely familiar to all: Egypt, Sumer, Assyria, Persia. Their stories are invariably given at the beginning of any world history narrative.

It is, however, beyond the scope of this book and the ability of this writer to go into detail about these highly romanticized histories. Instead, I propose to lay down broad strokes and then examine those significant points that have implications both within and beyond West Asia.

Let us consider the steady expansion of the scope of civilizations and states in the ancient Near East. While it may seem obvious, the spatial extent of rulership grew over time: Akkad expanded farther than the Sumerian city-states (c. 3000 B.C.), the ancient Babylonian Empire farther than Akkad, and the Assyrian Empire farther than Babylon.

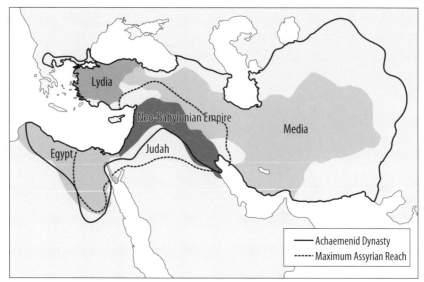

Fig. 6. The Achaemenid Dynasty and the Rise and Fall of the States of the Ancient Near East

Naturally, this also means that their respective civilizations were propagated and established to the extent of their domains and beyond, over periods of time more or less coincident with their rule. After establishing and disseminating its collective civilization, the ancient Near East reached its height during the ancient Persian and Alexandrian empires.

Next to consider is that, in the course of these expansions, their regional organizations were mostly clear-cut. While Persia conquered the whole of the ancient Near East, it was preceded by the mutual coexistence of Egypt, Lydia, Media, and Babylonia, states that roughly correspond to present-day Egypt, Anatolia (Turkey), Syria, and Iran. These four great spheres can be considered the medium-scale regional units which later constitute the region of the greater ancient Near East and West Asia. These pluralist regions were organized into a whole by the Achaemenid dynasty (550–330 B.C.).

Greece, Rome, and India

Lasting over two hundred years, the Achaemenid dynasty set an example for the rest of the world thereafter of how to rule a geographically wide-ranging, pluralistic land. The eastern military campaigns of its successor, Alexander the Great (356–323 B.C.), extended as far as India and Central Asia, hastening the eastward spread of the ancient Near East civilization.

A common misconception is that Alexander the Great, and by extension ancient Greece, was in conflict and competition on equal terms with Persia and the ancient Near East. This can be attributed to a fallacy originating in the historical view of Westerners who interpret the reporting of the Persian Wars in Herodotus' *The Histories* to suit themselves.

Were Greece considered to have had an adversary, it would have been Phoenicia, a part of the Persian Empire, rather than the whole thereof. Greece was founded under the strong influence of Phoenicia and struggled with it for mastery of the Eastern Mediterranean. Alexander the Great was merely the inheritor of the ancient Near East—specifically, Persia.

A similar situation occurred in the West. The rival of early Rome was Carthage, its enemy in the Punic Wars. Rome defeated Carthage, which was part of the Phoenician expansion, to claim the mantle of Mediterranean supremacy.

Hence, Greece and Rome are themselves the fruits of growth and expansion of the ancient Near East. The Roman Empire represented the integration of Greece and Phoenicia, and their offshoots, Rome and Carthage. It is appropriate to treat the resulting so-called Mediterranean civilization as an enlargement of Syria, itself within the ancient Near East. In other words, we may think of this Mediterranean civilization as part of the ancient Near East.

That being the case, the Mediterranean and the Roman Empire cannot be considered independent civilizations. And how much greater a mistake it would be to go so far as to treat them as forebears of Europe. These fallacies underpin the European identity and are distinct from the

Alexander the Great
Photo from Luisa Ricciarini/Bridgeman Images

objective historical facts of the time. These fallacies thus affected subsequent history and formed the basis for the modern world.

The Roman Empire constituted the western part of the divided ancient Near East civilization; Egypt, Anatolia, and Syria. The eastern part of the ancient Near East—Iran—was controlled by the Parthian dynasty (247 B.C.–224 A.D.) and thereafter by the Sasanian dynasty (226–651 A.D.). This split is best seen as contiguous with the breakup of the Alexandrian Empire.

It then becomes possible to interpret other civilizations similarly. From the Indus civilization to the unification of the Mauryan Empire (c. 321–185 B.C.), the course of the establishment of the civilization of India follows practically the same trajectory as that of the ancient Near East or the Roman Empire that diverged from it. At heart, the peoples of India were Aryan, as were the Persians (ancestors of modern Iranians), and they were all undoubtedly affected by waves from the ancient Near East.

The trajectory of Indian civilization can be divined from the strong traces of Iranian civilization and Zoroastrianism to be found in

Hinduism and Buddhism, which originated in India. The eastern ends of the ancient Near East, Persia, and the Alexandrian Empire fragmented into countries which then developed independently of one another, and the land of India has thereafter been continually buffeted by shocks and other impacts from its west.

From Central Asia to China

India was not the only land at the eastern end of these prior civilizations to be so affected. Another such region was the middle part of Central Asia, located between the Amu and Syr Rivers. Sogdians had long been established in this fertile oasis zone, and were influenced by the Iranian civilization, as seen by their devotion to Zoroastrianism. The land therefore came to be known as Sogdiana. And from this base, the Sogdians propagated the ancient Near East civilization even farther east, eventually founding the Huang He civilization.

Recent progress in archaeology has revealed that many civilizations coexisted in China in addition to the Huang He, such as the Chang Jiang (Yangtze River) civilization. It was the Huang He Basin civilization, however, that outlasted all others to form the core of the sphere where the Chinese writing system would later prevail, and thus the mainstream of Chinese history.

This region is frequently referred to in Chinese as "Zhongyuan" (central plains), though nowadays it may be more readily recognized as "Huabei" (Northern China). The former, however, has the meaning of "center," and the self-consciousness of this sense is critical in terms of the history of China. Hence, I propose to stick with it in this book.

Zhongyuan consists of both farmland and arid regions. Geographically speaking, much of it is plains. These conditions make it ripe for nomadic incursion. The Great Wall was thus necessary to thwart such attacks. In essence, Zhongyuan was a mixed region, lying at the boundary between nomadism and agriculture, and had the same location conditions as those found in the ancient Near East. Its history also closely parallels that of the ancient Near East and India. In the case of Zhongyuan, rival chieftains battled for supremacy over the land in the Spring and Autumn and the Warring States periods (770–221 B.C.), culminating in the Qin-Han unification.

While there is no unequivocal physical evidence of any connection between Zhongyuan and the ancient Near East, the existence and role of the Silk Road and Central Asia lead one to consider it unusual had there been no connection at all. By analogy with subsequent history, such a connection did exist: the regimes of the region consistently attempted to maintain ties with the so-called *seiiki*, or Western regions.

Some three hundred years passed between the unification of the ancient Near East under the Achaemenid dynasty and the unification of China under Qin Shi Huang (China's first emperor). Over this period, West, South, and East Asia at last came into line. That each of these achieved overall unification over a similar trajectory attests to the common foundation underlying their respective structures. What then happened after these unifications? Relations between these regions are at least as worthy of attention as their internal historical paths.

3. Migrations and the Demise of the Ancient Civilizations

Ages of "Collapse"

"The Roman Empire fell due to the migrations of the Germanic peoples."

This was history as it was taught to me in junior high school, in the 1970s. I haven't heard how the subject is taught nowadays.

As a factual historical process, this thesis is by no means mistaken. However, having read various historical texts over the intervening years, I have come to realize that it is a wholly insufficient explanation.

There are numerous areas of doubt. On the one hand, why was it necessary for the "Germanic peoples" to migrate, abandoning the places where they had been living in the process? And was it only they who did so, or were there other similar instances?

On the other hand, why did Rome decline and fall? At the time, as I recall, it was divided into Eastern and Western empires. Why do we speak of "the fall of the Roman Empire" when it was only its Western Empire that collapsed? For that matter, what do we mean by "collapse"? We're just getting started, and already we have many questions.

This phenomenon of invasive migration was happening along similar lines all across Eurasia. Zhongyuan was similarly being rent asunder at nearly the same time as the Western Roman Empire fell. The Han dynasty gave way to the Three Kingdoms, and while the Han was reunified for a time thereafter, it was promptly attacked by nomads. What, then, should we make of such collapses?

In this manner, the fourth and fifth centuries were a time of ruin and disintegration in both East and West Eurasia. And these episodes were likewise driven by the migrations and raids of nomadic and other tribes. The question then becomes, what brought about such a catastrophe?

Climatic Cooling

The possibilities seem endless. There are probably a variety of direct causal relationships based on time, place, and situation. In terms of the most pervasive and fundamental factor, however, a new answer has recently come to light: climatic fluctuation—in this case, climatic cooling on a global level.

Perhaps the problematic warming climate of recent decades makes the kind of climate change that occurred in these ancient times understandable to some extent. The problem, however, is that such climate change, whether cooling or warming, induces disasters and upsets or even wrecks ecosystems.

The impact of such cooling would, of course, vary by locale. It would probably be less problematic for a warm region to get cooler. A temperature drop in a warm place would not have serious implications for human survival—although there would still be noticeable effects on agriculture and production due chiefly to cold-weather damage. Over the long term, matters would become more dire.

The effect would be more pronounced in cold lands. Greater cooling frequently makes such places less viable for living things. Crops and grasslands already barely surviving might come to nothing. Diseases would more easily become epidemics. Life itself would be threatened. To survive, peoples living in cold interior regions, whether nomads or farmers, would migrate to even slightly warmer places. Many of the Germanic peoples had moved to areas within the bounds of the Roman Empire long before the so-called Migration period. Nor were they by any means the only such wanderers.

The "Migration period" refers to the time when bands of armed refugees, compelled to flee their homelands, entered the Roman Empire and made it their new home by force. This was a cascade, instigated by the movement and attacks of the nomadic Huns from far to the east. They were not the only peoples to travel such long distances, however. Everyone affected by global cooling had reason to leave.

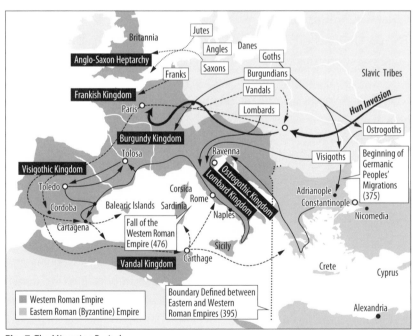

Fig. 7. The Migration Period

Hence, these migrations were not limited to this time period. Migrations from the north and the interior have repeated unabated ever since. In Europe alone there have been journeys by the Slavs, the Avars, and the Magyars from the east, as well as by the Normans from the north. And then there are the nomads of Central and East Asia, about whom I will have more to say later. The need for survival initially necessitated all of these movements.

New Structures

The nomadic world thus experienced a lifestyle crisis, while the agricultural world underwent a state of reduced production, destabilizing relations between the two. Commerce accordingly withered as well, given that its mainstay was the exchange of the products of both worlds. And conflict over scarce resources broke out inevitably and repeatedly.

In this way, both the nomadic and agricultural worlds felt the impact of global cooling. The resulting damage forced the nomads into either movement and raiding or migration and displacement. For their part, farmers not only had to forestall declining crop productivity but also cope with the aforementioned conflicts if they were to manage exiles and other newcomers.

Society itself had to change, from the forms of labor at the bottom to the power structures at the top. It became necessary to mobilize human power—by force, if necessary—via deforestation and cultivation for even the slightest increases in crop yield. The power of individuals who already had influence in such areas also grew as a consequence. The social situation became increasingly conducive to political factional struggles.

The ancient civilizations had arisen through the combination of nomads (military), farmers (production), and commerce (exchange). Global cooling upset the balance between these three, and the existing civilizations had no choice but to adopt new structures.

The Migration period represented one aspect of these processes. It can be seen as a trajectory which expressed these structural changes in much the same way as the large-scale regimes known as ancient empires all came to ruin and collapse.

Following the death of Alexander the Great, the ancient Near East had already split into a Mediterranean region extending from Syria westward and an eastern area with Iran at its center. The Roman Empire and Parthia had been at odds since their earliest periods, and both showed significant tendencies toward internal rivalries. The trend culminated in conflict between the Eastern Roman (Byzantine) Empire and Sasanian Persia, which began in the fourth century and continued thereafter.

Even so, the ancient Near East, with its longstanding civilization and warm climate, would not have been severely harmed by global cooling. Nor would its military-production-exchange balance have been seriously impaired. There were no significant instances of social displacement or political schisms. Both the Sasanian dynasty and the Eastern Roman Empire, which opposed each other across Syria and Egypt, were more or less politically and economically stable. One view is that this was the most advanced region of the time. And this may well be true, even if there is no way to measure and compare different areas in economic terms.

Fig. 8. The Dissolution of Zhongyuan in the Late 4th Century

In this sense, the regions hardest hit by global cooling were probably the fallen Western Roman Empire and Zhongyuan. Both were in cold lands far from, and more backwards than, the ancient Near East. Conversely, they were the archetypes of the crisis confronting the world at the time.

In particular, eastern and western agricultural spheres hit with the shock of the Migration period universally adopted ways of forcibly keeping refugees tied to their lands and making them cultivate it, in order to reduce fallow land as much as possible. The aim was to maximize labor in a harsh environment. This led to feudalism in Europe and the equal-field system (J. *kindensei*), in which agricultural lands were assigned to adult peasants for life, in East Asia. There seems to have been little difference between East and West in the underlying principle of forming close bonds between land and labor, regardless of how the systems that emerged might vary from one another.

Age of Religion and Faith

Then, as now, people turn to religion and faith when the stability of their livelihoods is in doubt and their survival at stake. This is not merely a crutch for individual attitude, morality, or living, either. It is inconceivable to cut oneself off from larger society if one is to make a living. Religious—faith-based—activities have an essential role in forming and preserving social order.

The farther back in time one goes, the more religion becomes entwined with politics and government. *Matsurigoto*, for example—classical Japanese for administration of government, now more commonly *matsuri*, referring chiefly to religious festivals—once had just such connotations, even when all was well. Such tendencies to cling to faith had to be further reinforced in times of crisis.

The once-flourishing ancient civilizations were at a loss in the face of climate change and the upheavals it caused. Reformations in faith and religion joined political and economic reform as one of the pillars that would support periods to come. It was no coincidence that the so-called world religions, including but not limited to Christianity and Buddhism, found opportunities to take root in this period. And the religion which brought this period to a close and pointed the way to a new one was Islam.

If religion and faith are taken to be supporters of social order, then religions should already have been founded when the ancient civilizations established their regional authority. And this was indeed the case, with Zoroastrianism in the ancient Near East and Persia, Brahmanism and early Buddhism in India, and Confucianism in China/Zhongyuan. It is necessary to note, however, that none of these are counted among "world religions."

"World Religions"?

The oldest, most widespread of these early religions was Zoroastrianism, which originated in ancient Persia. It spread from Rome in the West to India in the East. This is clear from the distinct traces left by this faith on such successor beliefs as Buddhism and Christianity. And if not only orthodox Zoroastrianism but also faiths that descended from it are included, such as Mithraism and the burgeoning Manichaeism, then Zoroastrianism reached as far as Central and East Asia, encompassing the whole of the continent. The trajectory of these religions also shows the course of the ancient Near East and Iranian civilizations proliferating, branching, and giving rise to other civilizations. Their dualistic good-versus-evil worldview also formed the basis of Judaism and Christianity, and thereby the wellspring of Western thought.

However, Zoroastrianism did not contribute to reestablishing order in different times when the political and economic environment and conditions had changed. Perhaps this was because it was ultimately an artifact suited to an earlier age. The creation of various sects or heresies such as Manichaeism might have been attempts to adapt to the changing times.

New religions were created that were even more widely adopted. These are what we now term "world religions."

Christianity is the supreme example of these. To put it another way, the very concepts of "religion" and "world" originate in the modern West, making them products of Eurocentrism. In modern times, Western

Christianity—meaning Catholicism and Protestantism—is the definition of "world religion." Other beliefs such as Buddhism and Islam, both adopted irrespective of ethnic boundaries in like manner to Christianity, were merely subsumed under the same heading. While the concept of "world religion" strikes me as problematic, I find myself without any apt alternative descriptors for purposes of this book. Thus, I appear to be stuck with it.

Along these lines, however, "world religions" emerged in the ancient Near East and South Asia, spreading eastward and westward from there. All "world religions" are products of Asian history. Defining the concept of "world religion" in terms of Eurocentrism is both ironic and prone to misunderstanding. We should examine the positioning and roles of these "world religions" without letting ourselves get distracted by such questions of definition.

Christianity, Rome, and the Ancient Near East

Christianity was born in Syria and Judea, the heart of the ancient Near East. And it spread first of all throughout the western part of the ancient Near East because the Roman Empire governed that region.

It was only natural, then, that the first devotees of Christianity came mostly from within the occupants of the ancient Near East, which was the eastern part of the Roman Empire. And the political center of gravity of the overall empire shifted to the east, which at the time was more culturally and economically advanced. There, in the early fourth century, Constantine the Great (272–337) gave official standing to Christianity. This and the founding soon after of Nova Roma, or Constantinople, were responses to the social and political circumstances of his time.

Constantine the Great
© NPL–De Agostini Picture Library/Bridgeman Images

If we broaden our field of view still farther, we find that the Christian Roman

Empire confronted Sasanian Persia, which had come to practice pure Zoroastrianism. This composition can be thought of as underscoring the schism of the ancient Near East in religious terms.

There were churches, of course, in the old imperial capital of Rome, where the Western Roman emperor ruled. The Western Roman lands took a different path, however, as the imperial line was extinguished in the course of the Migration period, while the Church of Rome survived.

Accordingly, the orthodoxy of Rome and Christianity would at least initially have been present in the Eastern Roman, or Byzantine, Empire, near the center of the ancient Near East. It is essential that this not be misunderstood. To treat Christianity as synonymous with Catholicism (i.e., the Church of Rome) or with the West is itself a Eurocentric preconception. There undoubtedly are historical processes that are appropriately seen in such terms. However, they correspond to times long after those under consideration at this point, and thus, discussions of them must be left to later in this book.

All of this shows that neither the old Zoroastrianism of the Sasanian dynasty nor the new Orthodox Eastern Roman Christianity succeeded in spanning the whole of the ancient Near East. Both were incapable of instituting a world order for the coming age. Such is the only conclusion that can be drawn from an Asian historical standpoint. One could say that a different faith and order were needed, neither Persian nor Roman, but a system of belief that encompassed both. And we must take care not to be carried away by the notion of a Catholic/Protestant "world religion."

East Asian Buddhism

Let us turn our gaze eastward, to a time nearly parallel with the establishment and proselytizing of Christianity. It is well known that Buddhism originated in the fifth century B.C., and that a myriad of variations was born from that initial early Buddhism through interpretations of dogma. Theravada Buddhism was transmitted from Sri Lanka to Southeast Asia and became established there before the time of the Mauryan Empire. It maintains a significant presence in Southeast Asia, even today.

In the time of crisis that has been our subject thus far, however, the introduction and spread across East Asia of the later Northern, or Mahayana, Buddhism demands our attention (see Fig. 9).

Unlike Theravada Buddhism, which emphasizes deliverance of the individual monk, Mahayana Buddhism preaches salvation for all living beings. From its origins around the start of the first millennium, Mahayana rapidly passed from present-day Afghanistan to China through Central Asia along the so-called Silk Road. Eventually it would reach the Korean Peninsula and the Japanese archipelago. This development was not merely a matter of personal belief but one that ultimately would influence the destiny of all East Asia.

As a folk religion of the Han Chinese there was Confucianism, which was indigenous to China and also served as the ideology of the Han

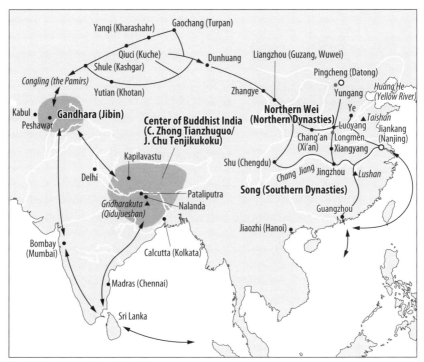

Fig. 9. The Introduction of Buddhism
Italicized names indicate geographic features.

Xuanzang
Photo courtesy of Tokyo National Museum.
(https://colbase.nich.go.jp/)

dynasty. This changed with the advent in China of Mahayana Buddhism, which was of a far higher order of abstraction than Confucianism. It was a world religion, with universality and a profound worldview that transcended tribal, ethnic, and regional conceptions.

Thus, Mahayana Buddhism spread rapidly during a period of political fragmentation beginning in the third century, following the collapse of the Han dynasty. It is no wonder that people facing a series of crises sought comfort in Mahayana Buddhism instead of Confucianism, whose doctrines were based solely in real-world relations.

In China/Zhongyuan, however, Confucianist doctrine and scripture had long since established the framework of thought and language in what is now considered classical Chinese. Investing this region with Buddhism would require rendering its sutras into Chinese as well, and so a massive translation project was initiated. Of particular renown in this regard are the accomplishments of Kumarajiva (344–413) and Xuanzang (602–664).

The Buddhist sutras play a significant role in Japanese life to this day, especially with regard to funerals, memorials, and *shakyo* (copying sutras by hand for training or meditative purposes). The sutras are all written in Chinese characters, without recourse to the kana syllabic writing systems that are also part of Japanese. Therefore, the Chinese forms of Buddhist expressions for such concepts as "omens" (J. *engi*), "worlds" (J. *sekai*), and "earthly passions" (J. *bonno*) have become embedded in the daily lives of the Japanese people. All of these notions that Japanese today take as givens originated in this much earlier epoch.

In this way, the sutras of India were introduced and adopted into China, a place completely different linguistically as well as culturally. They could not possibly have been imported in the original Sanskrit or any other Indian language. Mahayana Buddhism became the very substance of the cultural sphere of East Asia where the Chinese writing system prevailed because Chinese had been substituted for Sanskrit. Thus, it became possible to think of and hand down Mahayana Buddhism in Chinese instead. Similarly, Tibetan Buddhism flourished in the Tibetan Plateau owing to the translation of Buddhist scriptures into Tibetan.

Movements aimed at building a social order based on Buddhist ideology rose to prominence in China around the fifth century, during the period of its Northern and Southern dynasties. These regimes, based in Zhongyuan and Jiangnan, competed in demonstrations of their Buddhist faith. The magnificent World Heritage site of the Yungang Grottoes is associated with this period, as is a commonly known Tang poetry phrase that translates roughly as "480 Southern dynasty temples."

This dynastic competition over Buddhist practice established one of the driving forces that brought a new age of advancement to China, and indeed to East Asia as a whole, after so many disruptions. And the awakening of Japan would be one of the historical movements associated with this phenomenon.

CHAPTER 2

AGE OF MOBILIZATION

1. Reunification of East and West

Preeminence of the Ancient Near East

In the fifth and sixth centuries, the world saw the utter disruption of Zhongyuan and of the Western Roman Empire. As before, the center of gravity at the time remained in the ancient Near East. The Eastern Roman Empire and the Sasanian dynasty—which could be fairly described as the most advanced states—had split the region into east and west, and were thereafter engaged in a fierce contest of titans that neither side would yield.

Justinian, Eastern Roman (Byzantine) Emperor
Photo from History/Bridgeman Images

Both regimes were at their height around the same time as well. In the Eastern Roman Empire, it was the time of Emperor Justinian (483–565), who during his reign organized the structure of the state by such means as compiling the *Corpus juris civilis* and promoting the adoption of Christianity along with the purging of heretics and followers of other faiths. He was vital in external matters as well, conquering lost lands—thereby restoring most of the shape of the old Roman Empire and reunifying the Mediterranean world. This latter enterprise would prove to be a harbinger of the later Islamic dominion over the region.

Such enterprise was possible, however, precisely because it was unnecessary to be on guard against threats from the east. Justinian purchased peace by

Khosrow I, King of the Sasanian Dynasty of Persia
Photo from Granger/Bridgeman Images

Fig. 10. The Separation and Enlargement of the Ancient Near East (5th and 6th Centuries)

making annual payments to the Sasanian dynasty, his neighbors in that direction, indicating how dangerous they seemed to the Eastern Roman Empire. This was during the reign of King Khosrow I (r. 531–579), when the Sasanians were at their height.

In terms of policy, Khosrow's rule was like that of Justinian's. He oversaw the restructuring and reestablishment of Zoroastrianism, suppressed other new faiths including Manichaeism and Mazdakism, made further reforms to the military, and brought about domestic order. In external matters, he annihilated the Hephthalites, whose might had extended to the east through Central Asia and as far as northern India.

This was of a piece with Justinian's western campaigns. Khosrow, too, benefitted from rapprochement with the Eastern Roman Empire, as it enabled him to conduct his eastern battles without concern for his western flank. In this sense, he too was a forerunner of the Islamic conquest of Central Asia that occurred long after his time.

Persia and Rome thus expanded into their near east and near west, respectively (see Fig. 10). It is no exaggeration to say that they demonstrated the superiority of the ancient Near East.

But this expansion also was due to the fact that they were at peace with one another. Before long, however, both regimes would become embroiled in problems of succession, rending the peace between them and causing them to turn on each other instead.

In the early seventh century, Heraclius (c. 575–641), who became Eastern Roman emperor through a coup d'état, and Khosrow II (c. 570–628), grandson of Khosrow I, fought bloody wars repeatedly for more than twenty years. Initially, the Sasanians were triumphant. In 621, they occupied Syria, Egypt, and Anatolia, which had long been in Roman hands, and appeared to restore the scope of the ancient Achaemenid dynasty that had once unified the ancient Near East.

The Eastern Roman Empire, however, promptly counterattacked. Heraclius personally mounted a campaign that defeated the Sasanian forces at Nineveh in 627, then advanced on the Sasanian capital of Ctesiphon. The following year, Khosrow II was assassinated by his grandson Yazdegerd III (d. 651), forcing the Sasanian surrender.

Islam's Emergence and Triumph

This struggle of titans in eastern and western regions of the ancient Near East was a back-and-forth contest over Syria and Egypt. Even in the latter stages of the conflict, when it appeared that the Sasanians would overwhelm the Eastern Roman Empire, the latter rallied to restore the status quo. Both forces were exhausted.

Spreading outward to the south, the Arabian Peninsula is a desert where people have been living in nomadic ways and continue to do so even now. And at the time of the aforementioned conflict, a movement was getting started there that would change the course of world history.

Although largely desert, the area is not completely barren. Since the fifth century or thereabouts, the Sasanians had been settling the region, chiefly for mining development. Caravans traversed the land, and markets arose, as well as communities.

As hostilities between the Eastern Roman Empire and the Sasanians intensified, trade routes detoured south of their frontier, driving greater prosperity in the region. One of these booming merchant cities was Mecca.

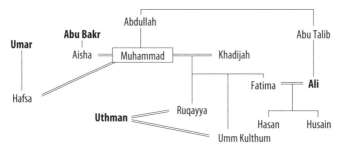

Fig. 11. Muhammadan Genealogy
The names of "perfect" or "rightly guided" caliphs are highlighted in boldface.
Double lines indicate relations by marriage.

Muhammad (c. 570–632) was a member of a prominent Meccan trading house. In 610, he had a monotheistic revelation that led to teachings he called Islam. Declaring himself a prophet, he proselytized his new religion. He gained many converts, including his wife Khadijah (555?–619), his cousin Ali (c. 600–661), and his friends Abu Bakr (c. 573–634) and Umar (d. 644).

Mecca, however, was sacred ground for polytheism, and those in power there persecuted Muslims, the Islamic faithful. In 622, Muhammad fled Mecca with his followers, moving to Yathrib, where he had long since been invited. This was the Hijrah, and Yathrib came to be known as Madinat-al-Nabi—the City of the Prophet—or in simpler language, Medina.

In 630, Muhammad captured Mecca, unifying the Arabian Peninsula. He died two years later. Islam's rise to power happened just as the Sasanian dynasty and the Eastern Roman Empire were locked in mortal combat and neither was paying attention elsewhere.

Muhammad's work was taken over by *khalifa*, or caliphs, "stand-ins" for the prophet, such as Abu Bakr and Umar. In particular, Umar, in his reign as the second caliph, organized the policy and framework of Islamic government. He established the Hijri calendar and created *sharia*, the Islamic system of legal practice. He also directed the Arab conquest, sending expeditionary forces against the exhausted Eastern Roman Empire and Sasanian dynasty.

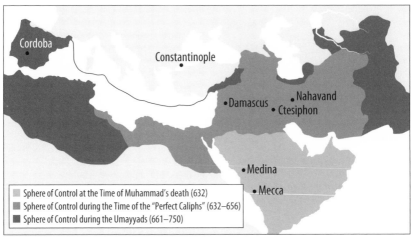

Fig. 12. The Spread of Islam and the Unification of the Ancient Near East
Islamic forces swallowed up the Sasanian lands and wrested away most of the Eastern Roman Empire. A comparison with Figure 10 shows that almost all of the ancient Near East was unified under Islam after the east-west split and expansion.

Umar began by conquering Syria in 635 and 636, then Egypt in 642. Heraclius's victory over the Sasanian dynasty thus came to nothing in little more than a decade. The Eastern Roman Empire, having lost the ancient Near East, its heart, saw its dominion reduced to only the Balkans and Anatolia.

The Sasanian dynasty, rival to the Eastern Roman Empire, met an even more wretched fate. Following the conquest of Syria, Islamic forces advanced eastward, occupying Ctesiphon in 637. In 642, after the conquest of Egypt, those forces invaded the Iranian Plateau and at Nahavand routed the Sasanian army that Yazdegerd III had assembled after fleeing his capital, effectively ending the Sasanian dynasty. Though Yazdegerd III fled east, making it as far as Merv in Khorasan, he was killed in 651, thus also ending the line of Sasanian kings.

Reunification of the Ancient Near East

Islam continued to expand. With the end of the so-called perfect or rightly guided caliphs after the death of Ali, the Umayyads who succeeded him moved their seat of power to Damascus. In addition to being the heart of commerce in the ancient Near East and the western terminus of the Silk Road, Syria was also the gateway to the Mediterranean. The Muslims, having thus far confined their jihad to land conquests, embarked at last on establishing their rule over the Mediterranean.

The crisis facing the Eastern Roman Empire was inescapable. While barely managing to defend Constantinople and its environs, as well as the Aegean and Adriatic seas, the empire had lost its dominions in Africa and the Iberian Peninsula. Consequently, command of the Mediterranean fell to the Muslims as well. It was even said that a Christian could not so much as float a single plank on the Mediterranean.

There is a tendency to interpret the preceding historical record as saying that the Mediterranean, an inland sea which had been inherently Roman (and by extension Christian and European), was stolen by the Muslims. It would be fair, however, to label such an inclination as Eurocentric.

Historically, Syria is inseparable from the Mediterranean. Greece and Rome were both products of Phoenician and Syrian expansion, and thus fundamentally part of the ancient Near East. Following the death of Alexander the Great, the ancient Near East from Syria westward parted ways with the region east of Persia, causing a schism in the so-called Mediterranean world as well.

Therefore, the Islamic Mediterranean conquest meant that the Mediterranean world was at last restored to the ancient Near East which lay to the east of the Mediterranean, and the sundered eastern and western portions once more integrated. Really, the event should be perceived as one in which the ancient Near East, after one thousand years of separation and expansion, achieved reunification under Islam.

The fact that Christian Rome stubbornly persisted would have tremendous significance in times to come. While this should not be overlooked, it must also not be mistaken for the Mediterranean situation at the time of the Islamic conquest.

The Entrenchment of Islam

Islam expanded through declarations of jihad (i.e., by military might). But it does not seem reasonable that Islam grew solely by use of force. It is important to keep in mind that Islam replaced a myriad of preexisting faiths and moral systems, including Christianity and Zoroastrianism, which were accepted across much of the ancient Near East, with a single system of order.

As with Christianity and Buddhism, a detailed examination of Islamic dogma is beyond the scope of this book. In brief, however, in its rejection of idolatry and denial of miracles, it was the most rational teaching of its time. Islam also taught that all people were equal human beings before Allah, the one God, with neither distinction between sacred and profane nor discrimination on the basis of rank. The formation of such a humanitarian community could supply a fresh morality and maintain strict discipline. It seems clear that to the people of the ancient Near East, Islam held attractions surpassing those of all existing religions.

Otherwise, Islam could hardly have proliferated in the twinkling of an eye as it did, nor remain entrenched to this day. In that sense, Islam could be said to be a universal system of order capable of encompassing a vast area, one which having emerged, veritably embodied the hopes and expectations of the entire ancient Near East at the time.

As with the religions that preceded it, Islam formed a bond among its adherents, becoming a part of all aspects of their lives, whether of language, faith, social etiquette, or politics. This remains more or less true even now, with rules prescribing everything from local daily life to external relations including warfare.

Perhaps an example at the most fundamental level will make this situation easier to understand. Given that the Koran, the Islamic scripture, is made up of entries in Arabic, it has had a decisive impact on the characters (i.e., the written language). It was at this time that the arrangement of written characters in the ancient Near East was ultimately defined as horizontal from right to left. By contrast, in the West, where Islam's reach did not extend, writing horizontally from left to right was made the rule by Christianity.

The Position of Central Asia

After sweeping over North Africa, Islam advanced into the Iberian Peninsula, which was subsumed under Islamic rule for the next several centuries. In crossing the Pyrenees and advancing farther north, however, the Muslim army was defeated by the Frankish kingdom in 732 between the towns of Tours and Poitiers. In this way, the Christian world barely managed to defend and secure the lands north of the Pyrenees.

Having thus been thwarted in the west at Constantinople and at the Pyrenees, Islam similarly failed to extend its influence beyond the Amu River, which marked the limit of its eastern campaigns. The boundaries of Islamic lands were thus established, for a time.

Beyond the Amu, in Central Asia, the Sogdians, a people of Iranian descent, were thriving. Central Asia—known as Sogdiana at the time—was one of the world's great commercial zones. It was the core of the Silk Road, and oasis cities were strung along its length. The Sogdians who lived there engaged in wide-ranging commerce from east to west, amassing wealth in the process. They commanded the world economy of the time.

The Turkic khaganate (Tujue), extending its might from the east, exercised political and military control over Sogdiana. The state was founded by nomads of Turkic origin who had been allies of the Sasanians when the latter defeated the Hephthalites in Central Asia.

Between the Sogdians and the Turkic khaganate, a cooperative relationship came into sharp focus in which commercial economic power was combined with nomadic military force. It might well be termed the prototype for such arrangements.

Peoples of the ancient Near East moved into the region from the west, fleeing the Islamic defeat of the Sasanians. They consisted of many ethnicities and religions: among them were Zoroastrians, Manichaeans, and Nestorians, the last of these having been declared heretics by the Eastern Roman Empire. In times to come, the business and missionary work of all of these would be roused to new life together with that of the Sogdians whom these various peoples found in the Sogdiana region. This could be said to be another reverberation of Islam's reunification of the ancient Near East.

Nor was that all. The Turkic khaganate who reigned in Sogdiana themselves would soon be upset. In addition to internal strife, a menace from far to the east was upon them. That menace was the might of the Tang, who based themselves in Chang'an, part of Zhongyuan.

From the Turkic Khaganate to the Sui and Tang Dynasties

A vast grassland extends from the northern part of East Asia, and the most prominent land in those grasslands is the Mongolian Plateau. And mighty nomadic states have arisen there throughout history. The Xiongnu, who troubled the Qin and Han dynasties which unified Zhongyuan, are the best-known case. The Turkic khaganate at this time had grown to a comparable scale.

In the mid-sixth century, the Turkic khaganate replaced another nomadic state, the Rouran khaganate, to control the Mongolian Plateau. From there, it wasted no time in extending its power, threatening Zhongyuan to its east and holding sway over Central Asia to its west. Perhaps due to their power growing too far, too fast, the Turkic khaganate split into east and west in some thirty years. Parallel to this development, a movement occurred to its near east in Zhongyuan, China, which could not be ignored.

With the onset of climatic cooling beginning in the third century, as described in Chapter One, northern nomads surged in waves into Zhongyuan, where settled agricultural peoples had superior population ratios. There, the nomads provoked great disorder. In the Chinese of the time, the agricultural peoples were known as Han, and the nomads as Hu.

With superior force of arms, the Hu dominated the numerically superior Han. They established one ruling regime after another, though they were not very successful at building stable systems. This was because the worldview and order of the ancient Qin-Han empires were no longer viable, and it was a challenge to devise a new political system to replace that worldview and order. To do so would take trial and error over a long period in Zhongyuan, which became the crucible for the Hu and the Han.

Both peoples studied their respective strengths and weaknesses and searched for ways to allocate roles between them. They eventually arrived at the Northern dynasty, founded by the Tuoba clan of the Xianbei tribe, which unified Zhongyuan in the first half of the fifth century. Succeeded by the Sui and Tang dynasties, this regime was the beginning of a polity in which the Hu and the Han could coexist as one.

The Xianbei were another long-established nomadic people of the Mongolian Plateau. Migrating south to Zhongyuan, they were forced to confront and compete with the Rouran and the Turkic khaganates for supremacy, as they had on the Mongolian Plateau. They were the emperors of the Han and also the *khagans*, or sovereigns, of the nomads, which put them in the position of contending for power.

For this reason, the vicissitudes of the Turkic khaganate had a tremendous impact on the political situation in Zhongyuan and East Asia. The

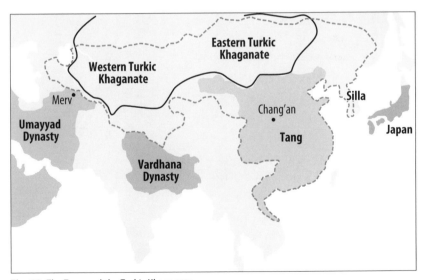

Fig. 13. The Tang and the Turkic Khaganate
The dashed line indicates the farthest extent of the Tang.

Northern dynasty of the Tuoba was forced to submit when the Turkic khaganate was at its height. The balance of power was inverted, however, when the Turkic khaganate split into east and west, and Zhongyuan was instead unified under the Sui and Tang dynasties and merged with the Southern dynasty. At the beginning of the seventh century, it was the Turkic khaganate that repeatedly found itself in the inferior position.

The Tang and Central Asia

Taizong (Emperor) Li Shimin (598–649), de facto founder of the Tang, embodied these chaotic times. Whereas the Tang imperial household presented itself to the Han as having a bloodline of impeccable Han purity deriving from Li of the Longxi, an illustrious aristocrat, it really originated with an entirely different tribe: the aforementioned Tuoba clan of the Xianbei. Accordingly, the Tang *taizong* was the Son of Heaven who balanced the Hu and the Han relative to one another and who also possessed superior military prowess. In 630 he subjugated the Eastern Turkic khaganate, raised his military prestige for all to see, and was proclaimed *tengri khagan* (khan of Heaven). The following generation moved still farther west in the latter half of the seventh century and defeated the Western Turkic khaganate as well, extending the power of the Tang as far as Central Asia.

Nor would the Tang overlook the economic and commercial might of Sogdiana, which the Turkic khaganate had leveraged. The Tang controlled the trading activities of the Sogdian merchants, leveraged those activities

Li Shimin, Taizong (Emperor) of the Tang
Photo courtesy of National Palace Museum, Taipei.
(https://theme.npm.edu.tw/opendata/)

in military affairs, and drew the Sogdian merchants into Zhongyuan as well. Thus, the Central Asian economy, which from the outset had had a strong relationship with the ancient Near East, was also connected with East Asia from the west, along a vector opposite to that of the expansion of the Tang.

Chang'an was the point of contact. This base of the unified Hu-Han regime became an important hub of the Silk Road, and commerce and culture shone brightly. The core was Iranian culture, of which the Sogdian merchants formed the vanguard. In terms of religion, it is note-worthy that Zoroastrianism, Manichaeism, and Nestorianism, all of which originated in the ancient Near East, were introduced in the region at this time.

Japanese historian Ishida Mikinosuke (1891–1974) observes the follow-ing in his noted work *Choan no haru* (Springtime in Chang'an):

A respectable number of *seiko* who revered the Son of Heaven of the Great Tang as *tengri kaghan* gathered around Khumdan, the capital of Tamghaji, for trade benefits.

"Tamghaji" was the name given to Zhongyuan, China, by the peoples of Central Asia and the ancient Near East, and "Khumdan" refers to Chang'an Castle. It appears that the former is a corruption of the Tuoba "Tabɣač," and the latter a corruption of *jing cheng*, meaning "capital." *Seiko* refers to "traders from *seiiki*" (Western regions), particularly the Sogdian merchants.

The eastern and western parts of Asia, which had long been thrown into chaos by climatic cooling, regained a measure of stability through the establishment of the new, wide-ranging Islam and Tang systems of order, which were unlike the ancient civilizations. Of course, this would not be the end of the matter, and a new historical period seemed imminent.

2. East and West Asia: Migrations and Divisions

"East Asia" and "East Eurasia"

The Chinese character for "Tang" holds particular significance for Japanese. The Japanese embassies to Tang dynasty China, with their implied ancient exoticism, are also well known in this context. At one time the character for "Tang" signified "China" itself. When combined with certain other characters, it was used to indicate "India," which in time came to mean "foreign lands" or "faraway places"; when used with a character for "person," it could denote either "Chinese" or the general concept of "foreigner."

Furthermore, Japan had only recently been established as a country in the Tang period. From the perspective of Japan at the time, being such a small country, the Tang (i.e., China) was overwhelmingly large and advanced—a foreign land that seemed to be the whole world. Things from outside Japan—whether from China or elsewhere—thus came to be named generically in Japanese with expressions including this character. Examples include Japanese words for chili peppers, sweet potatoes, and corn. A term whose characters literally mean "hairy foreigner," once commonly used to mean "Westerner," was eventually considered discriminatory and has long been abandoned.

All of these are highly commonplace sensibilities and expressions in Japanese that, restated in historical terms, constitute a concept known as the "East Asian world." This idea, proposed by historian Nishijima Sadao (1919–1998), is a conception of a historical picture of East Asia overall, with the Tang tributary system at its core. It too has long been part of common usage in the field of Japanese historical studies, where it is often referred to as the Nishijima hypothesis.

Of course, the Tang system of order, with its large scope, involved more than just Japan and the Japanese. It constituted a sphere that brought together countries and groups along its periphery as a magnet attracts iron filings, a sphere that had a single great cultural assemblage. The Korean Peninsula and the Japanese archipelago in particular were profoundly influenced in the fundamentals of language, culture, and institutions by the Chinese characters, Buddhism, and the political system of *ritsuryosei*, adopted from the Tang *lüling* (government of law) system. The pull of Zhongyuan would continue to make itself felt on these countries as well.

There is nothing wrong with this summary of the "East Asian world" concept. But there is more to it. Alone, it makes for an inadequate description of the Tang. It is an artifact of the blinkered perspective and sensibility of the Japanese, a people located as far to the east as it is possible to be. The Tang had crucial aspects that the Japanese tend not to notice. In fact, the focus of the Tang's own interests was, if anything, not on its eastern but its western flank.

As we have seen, the infusion of the more advanced Iranian culture, and the movements and attitudes of the nomadic world, with its superior force of arms, defined the regime and institutions of the Tang. That "East Asian world" that Japanese chiefly perceive, with its overemphasis on the spheres of East Asia, including the Japanese archipelago, where the Chinese writing system prevailed, is accordingly becoming increasingly obsolete in academic circles.

"East Eurasia" is a term frequently invoked as a replacement concept. It can be thought of as an expression more conscious of links with the West and the nomads, referring geographically to a range which links East Asia with Central Asia. At one time, the Tang integrated the whole of this East Eurasia region (see Fig. 13, p. 75).

The Place of Buddhism in the Scheme of Things

While the Tang distinguished themselves in feats of arms for a time, as a system which would integrate a region on the scale of East Eurasia, the dynasty was far more brittle and lacking in permanence than Islam to the west. One reason may be that it was unable to build a societal organization and a system of order that presented universal values that could be adopted in common across a wide region, as Islam had done.

If there were something that occupied such a position in the East, it would be Buddhism, which spread from India along the Silk Road to

Zhongyuan, and from there to the Korean Peninsula and the Japanese archipelago—indeed, the whole of East Eurasia. Already holding sway in Zhongyuan, Buddhism gained converts in various instances among adherents of other religions who migrated there from Central Asia, such as the Sogdians.

Japanese readers would likely find more compelling the case of how Buddhism came to Japan. The *Zuisho Wakokuden* (The Book of Sui: Record of Japan) contains a famous diplomatic message from Prince Shotoku (first ruler over a unified Japan, seventh century) to the emperor of China, which may be rendered in more or less modern language as "The Son of Heaven of the Land of the Rising Sun sends this message to the Son of Heaven of the Land of the Setting Sun, in hopes that all is well with you." It is also written there that the messenger who delivered the message added a verbal remark, which may be similarly rendered as "I send my emissary to your presence, Bodhisattva Son of Heaven to the west across the sea, as fellow worshipers of Buddhism." In other words, a messenger was being expressly dispatched to the Sui emperor, being the "Bodhisattva Son of Heaven" who had revived Buddhism. It is, of course, unknown whether this statement was actually made. At the very least, however, there was a situational awareness on the part of the Zhongyuan regime that recorded these words that the state in the archipelago sought to form a relationship of attachment with the Son of Heaven on the grounds that it too believed in Buddhism.

Dreams of a Buddhist Empire

Perhaps because of this awareness, there were attempts to build a wide-ranging universal system of order out of Buddhism as well. Notable cases include Emperor Wendi (541–604) of the Sui dynasty (late sixth through early seventh centuries) and Empress Wu Zetian (624–705) some one hundred years later. Each compared themselves to the *cakravartin* (one whose wheel turns everywhere; i.e., a universal ruler who rules without force), in attempting to build what might be called a Buddhist empire.

Emperor Wendi of the Sui was the ruler who united the polities known as the Northern and Southern dynasties. He probably became a pious Buddhist as much out of political necessity as personal faith. It would have represented an effort to find a universal embodiment of a higher order to fulfill and maintain the integration of these dynasties, which were steeped in Buddhism.

As for Wu Zetian, she was the empress who inherited the Tang's East Eurasian integration and assumed command of the regime. Preserving that integration involved her enthronement as empress, which was beyond the pale of the political traditions of the Zhongyuan classical Chinese sphere that were rooted in Confucianist thought. Hence, she likely sought a more universal ideology and system of order.

There is no evidence that either attempt was achieved and thus entrenched. The Sui dynasty was supplanted by the Tang, and the designs of Wu Zetian were rejected by the Tang emperor Xuanzong (685–762). Buddhism in East Eurasia was not universalized, integrated into society, or systematized, as Islam was in the ancient Near East and the Mediterranean.

The An-Shi Rebellion

This failure to instill Buddhism may have been one of the reasons for the sudden decline of the order, stability, peace, and prosperity which had depended on the Tang. Following its peak in the first half of the eighth century, with the reign of Xuanzong, the dynasty rapidly collapsed. The event that precipitated the fall of the Tang was the so-called An-Shi Rebellion of 755.

As the name suggests, this disturbance was fomented by An Lushan (c. 705–757) and Shi Siming (c. 703–761), both of whom were generals of *seiko*, or peoples foreign to the Tang—offspring of mixed Sogdian and Turkic parentage. As a result, the forces they commanded were chiefly drawn from the Turkic cavalry.

The foundation of the unified Hu-Han scheme of the Tang lay in the long-standing equal-field system (J. *kindensei*) and the military levy on the peasantry known as *fubing* (J. *fuheisei*). These systems, part of the Tang *ritsuryosei* political system adopted by Japan, had the objective of maximizing the labor of peasant farmers by dealing with them individually, and thereby directly resourcing food production and warfare. And they underpinned the national strength of the Northern dynasty, the Sui, and the Tang.

As the Tang expanded, however, these systems could not manage large areas, as they were devised for use with a segment of the agricultural populace, and they began to break down. The military resorted instead to recruiting soldiers, with nomads forming the mainstay.

The army of An Lushan was the exemplar. It was tasked with maintaining order from the plains to the grassland belts that were part of a large and strategic territory north of the Huang He. In geopolitical terms, it is particularly significant that the army of An Lushan was based in this area, given that present-day Beijing was founded there.

The Dissolution of "East Eurasia"

The military strength of the Tang at this time was configured more or less along these lines. As the Hu-Han unification in Zhongyuan was the raison d'être of the Tang, this transformation of the military system—employing the Sogdians, the Turkic peoples, or cavalry—can be said to be an expression and a part of the system that was suited to the times. And somehow, order was maintained and integration of "East Eurasia" preserved thereby, until the first half of the eighth century.

The An-Shi Rebellion was, accordingly, not simply civil unrest or war. It symbolized the systemic collapse of the Tang.

The impact on the internal Hu-Han unification, to say nothing of the external scope of East Eurasia, was tremendous. Triggered by the An-Shi Rebellion, the Uyghur khaganate, which was established on the Mongolian Plateau by one of the Turkic ethnic groups, and Tibet (Tufan), on the Tibetan Plateau, increased in power, putting pressure on the Tang. Nor was that all. Having once escaped Tang control, the rebel forces, with a stronger inclination toward independence, fought everywhere among themselves, resulting in the breakup of territory as far as the interior of Zhongyuan.

It was no longer possible to effectively manage the plurality of peoples and forces of East Eurasia, Zhongyuan included, with the structure and

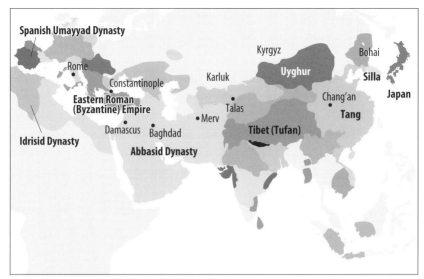

Fig. 14. The World in the Latter Half of the 8th Century

system of order of the Tang. It would not be easy to find a new system of order, however. East Asia therefore entered into another era of rioting and trial and error.

From the Umayyads to the Abbasids

The West could be said to have a somewhat higher degree of stability than the East. In the mid-eighth century, around the time of the An-Shi Rebellion in Zhongyuan, the Umayyad dynasty fell. It was succeeded by the Abbasid dynasty, under whose rule the Islamic sphere as a whole, which encompassed the ancient Near East, preserved a scale nearly equal to the preceding era and gloried in its might and prosperity for another century.

The inclinations of the Umayyad and Abbasid dynasties differed. The former, with its foundation and center rooted in Syria, sought to command the Mediterranean and integrate the ancient Near East on an east-west vector. Thus, it focused on and showed favoritism toward the rising Arabs who encountered the other tribes conquered by the Umayyads.

By contrast, the Abbasids shifted their center of gravity to command of the land route—the Silk Road—even as they inherited their predecessors' sphere of activity. That they moved their capital from Damascus to Baghdad makes this clear. The dynasty's vector turned from west to east, toward the Iranian Plateau. The intent was to take over the legacy of the ancient Persian civilization, with which many tribes had been involved.

If the Umayyad dynasty was western-oriented and Arab in nature, then the Abbasid dynasty turned toward the east and Persia. And for a while, the latter enjoyed great success. The ninth century was the heyday of the Abbasids, producing the gorgeous golden age of Islamic culture exemplified by the *Arabian Nights*.

At this time, the ancient writings of Persia, Greece, India, and Syria were collected on a grand scale and translated into Arabic, bringing together the very best of ancient science and literature. This initiative would form the basis of the Renaissance yet to come.

The Islamic World Becomes Multipolar

The Umayyad dynasty, being the first hereditary Islamic state, lasted for a hundred years or so. The succeeding Abbasid dynasty had a much longer lifespan, surviving for some five hundred years. Its rule, however, was not uniformly efficacious or stable across the whole of its existence. Cracks began to appear over time between its eastern and western territories. These could be thought of as side effects and new developments brought about by the dynasty's change of attitude.

One such crack was the relaxing of the Abbasids' command of the West—specifically, the Mediterranean. The distant Iberian Peninsula was not the only place where a schism occurred in the successor state of the Umayyads. The Maghreb was next to secede, and eventually even Egypt—the nearest and most crucial state—also broke away from the regime's control. In this way, the center of the Islamic world began changing into a multipolar region. This state of affairs was symbolized and decided by the conquest of Egypt and the establishment of Cairo in the tenth century by the Fatimid dynasty, which was implacably hostile to the Abbasids. Egypt and Cairo remain to this day a prime center of the Arab world and Islam.

Even more important than the Mediterranean theater was the East. The strong interest that the Abbasids had from the outset in Central Asia was evident in their eastern-facing empire. Soon after their state was founded, they found themselves in conflict over Central Asia with the Tang forces. Hostilities broke out in the Battle of Talas in 751, which ended in Islamic victory. Sogdiana, which had been connected to the East from the time of the Turkic khaganate to the Tang, would thereafter turn westward, returning to the ancient Near East and becoming part of its jurisdiction once more.

From the standpoint of controlling the main artery of the Silk Road and seizing control of world trade, the recapture of Sogdiana was a major accomplishment for the ancient Near East. The central Abbasid regime would, however, have to maintain a position of political and military dominance if they were to continue to have their fill of the fruits of this feat. Before long, a momentous event would occur in Central Asia to largely upend the state of affairs there.

Persia and Central Asia

The sphere of the Persian civilization and language, where the Iranians and the Sogdians lived, spans the region from the Iranian Plateau across the Amu River to Central Asia. Even after the Sasanian dynasty was destroyed and the region subjugated by the Muslims, the Iranians and the Sogdians were never likely to be completely submissive to the Arabs, whom they considered upstarts. These people had a history of, and pride in, having ruled the ancient Near East. In reaction to the Arab-first policies of the Umayyads, the Sogdians nurtured the minority Shia sect of Islam, eventually giving impetus to the rise of the Abbasids.

Once the Abbasids had seized power, however, and come to terms with the orthodox Sunni—inheritors of the Umayyads—the Shia and other betrayed parties began operating from Iran and points east. Such pressures thus acted mightily on the Abbasids, who had no choice but to orient themselves eastward if only to forestall defections by those whom they had betrayed. Their declining political and military influence and power, however, could not constrain such moves toward reaction and separation.

In the early half of the tenth century, with their grip on the Mediterranean weakening, and also preceded somewhat by the conquest of Egypt by their great rivals the Fatimids, the Abbasids were also confronted by a massive change in their eastern lands. The Buwayhids, a Shia state, rose to power in a region with Fars at its heart. Their power grew, and soon they were in Baghdad. Under the Buwayhids, the caliph of Baghdad was reduced to being more or less a puppet ruler, with real power in the hands of the Buwayhids. Thereafter, the caliph effectively became a figurehead, and the Abbasids ceased to exist as a governing power for all intents and purposes.

Farther to the east, however, a situation of greater interest had been evolving for quite some time. A half-century earlier, in the latter half of the ninth century, the Samanid dynasty had established itself from the even more remote Khorasan to Sogdiana. Though Iranian, the Samanids recognized the authority of the Abbasids in Baghdad, and in fact went so far as to present themselves as a bulwark on the eastern border of the Abbasid dynasty. Hence, the Samanid dynasty occupied a completely different position from that of the later Buwayhid dynasty, despite the Iranian origins of both.

Of particular note is the role played by the Samanid dynasty in the Islamization of Sogdiana and Central Asia as a whole. The religiously disordered Sogdiana became Islamic beginning in the tenth century, and the land was thereafter called Ma Wara al-Nahr ("that which lies beyond the river") in Arabic, or Transoxania. This development is also meaningful in that it indicated that the land was no longer that of the Sogdians.

The Turkification of the Uyghurs and Central Asia

Following their Turkic predecessors, the Uyghurs rose up on the Mongolian Plateau to form the Uyghur khaganate, a nomadic empire, beginning in the mid-eighth century. Like the Turkic khaganate, they were a nomadic tribe of Turkic origin. While supporting the imperiled Tang in the An-Shi Rebellion, the Uyghur khaganate achieved a position of superiority and would glory in its own might and prosperity for some one hundred years. In the early half of the ninth century, however, the empire was attacked by the Kyrgyz from the north and collapsed.

The Uyghur people scattered at this time. It is said that the greatest number, exceeding 100,000, fled westward. They moved to the region of oases of the Tarim Basin south of the Tian Shan mountains, where their influence had already reached. There they established a settled lifestyle, founding the Uyghur kingdom of Qocho near the end of the ninth century.

This area, containing the eastern half of Central Asia, had been largely occupied up to then by Sogdian settlers of Iranian descent. The Turkic Uyghurs put down roots and coexisted with the Sogdians, becoming intertwined with them, and thus "Turkifying" the region by the thirteenth century, turning it into a land where Turkic was spoken on a day-to-day basis.

Other Uyghurs went even farther west, merging with the Karluks—another Turkic people, who lived at the northern base of the Tian Shan range—to found a new entity, the Karakhanid dynasty, notable for being the first Turkic Islamic polity. Many Turkic peoples ruled by the Karakhanid dynasty converted to Islam in the mid-tenth century, influenced by their western neighbor, the Samanid dynasty.

Fig. 15. The Islamic Sphere in the Latter Half of the 10th Century

The Spread of Islamization and Turkification

Turkic nomads had been moving into Central Asia, west of the Pamirs, into Sogdiana, since the emergence of the Turkic khaganate. The Turkic nomads' bonds with Islam were forged when the Abbasids brought these nomads under their influence. This was exemplified in the Turkic nomads being used as mamluks—slaves or soldiers—because of their strong martial temperament and proficiency in nomadic combat on horseback.

In response to the demand in the Islamic countries of West Asia, even farther west than their own domain, the Samanids enthusiastically employed mamluks and supplied them to that part of the world. The Samanids themselves also had a great number of mamluks, appointing them as bodyguards to the rulers as well as officers and troops in outlying regions. Their task was to ward off attacks by Turkic nomadic forces from the east. In effect, Turkic peoples ended up fighting each other.

With the defeat and fall of the Samanids at the hands of the Karakhanids in the late tenth century, Central Asia east and west of the Pamirs came under the domination of Turkic forces, increasing Turkification there. Sogdiana, land of the Sogdians, had by this time come to be called "Turkistan," which means "land of the Turkic people" in Persian. The name remains to this day. The Islamization of the Turkic peoples progressed further under the influence of the Karakhanids.

Although the region became more Turkic, the preexisting Iranian culture was never eradicated. It remained particularly strong in West Turkistan, where Persian-speaking people have survived to modern times. Consequently, the region stands in stark contrast to Turkistan east of the Pamirs, where the only language heard is Turkic—attesting to the tenacity of the geographically adjacent Persian civilization.

The Westward Advance of the Nomads

The two forces of Islamization from the west and Turkification from the east crossed swords at Ma Wara al-Nahr (Transoxania). This region, absorbing energy from both forces, made its dramatic appearance at a focal point in world history.

First on the scene were the Seljuks, formed of nomadic Turkic bands who had been subject to the Karakhanids. The Seljuks had lived for a long time near the Aral Sea, in the northern part of Central Asia. Then, after the Karakhanids overthrew the Samanid dynasty, the Seljuks moved southward en masse, eventually resettling near Bukhara. They were of course fervent believers in Islam.

Nor did their movements stop there, either. Eventually, the Seljuks moved westward across the Amu River, where they founded a polity that incorporated nomadic tribes that were said to number as many as ten thousand tents. In 1055, the Seljuk dynasty at last made its way to hegemony over the Islamic world by triumphantly entering Baghdad, officially claiming the title of sultan from the Abbasid caliphs, and overthrowing the Shia Buwayhid dynasty.

The Seljuk dynasty is especially renowned for having fought in the Crusades. This phenomenon of westward advance by the Turkic peoples was seen as a more or less universal practice at the time, a movement that can be described as flowing with the tide of the era.

The Turkic peoples were not the only ones moving in this fashion. Further nomadic migrations from east to west began gaining in momentum, as if following on the heels of the Turkic peoples. These waves would form the undercurrent of Asian history from the eleventh century onward.

3. Turkification and Khitan

The Uyghur as Focal Point

Beginning in the ninth century, East and West Asian history entered a time in which the respective periods of unification—of East Asia by the Tang dynasty and of West Asia by Islam—drew to a close, with both powers undergoing either disintegration and schism, or multipolarization. Energetic migration of nomadic forces spanning East and West Asia, especially the Turkic nomads, affected these changes.

The long westward movement of Uyghurs was the first instance and the centerpiece of such migration. In addition to their impact on the Central Eurasian civilization, which was configured from grassland and oasis cities, the agricultural sphere also felt their presence. These Uyghurs would influence the course of Asian history thereafter through actions beyond their nomadic movements.

Originally living a nomadic lifestyle on the Mongolian Plateau, the Uyghurs experienced a change first and foremost by settling in Central Asia. At the same time, however, they changed the nature of their established society there, through Turkification.

Even in terms only of polities known to be directly involved in this transformation, we have the Uyghur kingdom of Qocho and the Karakhanid dynasty as exemplars. Generally speaking, these states can be conceived as occupying the eastern and western parts of Central Asia, respectively. The Pamirs formed the boundary between them. The Uyghur kingdom of Qocho was oriented eastward, engaging with East Asia, and the Karakhanid dynasty turned westward, being connected with West Asia.

The Uyghurs and the Sogdians

At face value, "Turkification" means that the Sogdians of Iranian descent, who had been the dominant presence in Central Asia, had disappeared and become Turkic. This is not meant to suggest that one group of people was replaced by another the way one might repaint a wall.

From their homelands in Central Asia, the Sogdians had long controlled commercial rights over the whole of the Silk Road, the oases, and the grasslands. They engaged in wide-ranging commerce, trafficking between the agricultural and nomadic worlds and gaining entry to both.

In the process, more than a few of the Sogdians went from settled to nomadic lifestyles, from merchants into warriors. An Lushan, who made his power felt in Zhongyuan, in East Asia, is a case in point.

Gifted with flexibility and adaptability, the Sogdians operated over a wide area. In turn, the migrating Uyghurs dominated the Sogdians.

Turkic likely became the common tongue. This situation may itself have been a sign of Sogdian adaptability. After all, the Uyghurs embraced local social customs and put down roots, rather than the other way round. The Uyghurs were assimilated into the Sogdians and adopted their traditional modes of behavior.

One example of such acculturation was the Uyghur kingdom of Qocho, which had its domains in the eastern half of Central Asia. Located roughly where Xinjiang is in present-day China, it was also referred to as East Turkistan in its early days. This kingdom was known for adopting Buddhism and Manichaeism as well as for creating the Uyghur system of writing. This regime too can be seen as having embraced traditional Sogdian culture.

In this regard, the label "Uyghurs of Sogdian descent," coined by historian Moriyasu Takao (b. 1948), is fitting (Moriyasu, *Shiruku Rodo to To teikoku: Kobo no sekaishi 05* [The Silk Road and the Tang Empire: What Is Human History? vol. 5]). These people would become ever more busily engaged in East Asia, primarily farther east of their domain, the Uyghur kingdom of Qocho.

In East Asia, the term "Sogdian" had once been a byword for merchants and fortune, when the Sogdians had managed the economic arena. In those days, the Chinese word for "Sogdian" was instantly associated with "rich person" in people's minds. The Chinese expression *qiong Bosi*, for "poor Persian," was commonly understood in Zhongyuan to mean "unthinkable." In times to come, "Uyghur" would replace that phrase, itself becoming the byword for commerce and wealthy merchants instead.

The Realities of Turkification and Islamization

What was the situation in western Central Asia? The Karakhanid dynasty was the state where the Uyghurs seemed to exert tremendous influence west of the Pamirs. According to some sources, we find that the westward-moving Uyghurs had joined with the Karluks, a firmly rooted Turkic nomadic power. Although some uncertainties remain, this dynasty clearly arose where the Uyghurs arrived after their long westward migration. And as with the Uyghur kingdom of Qocho, the impact of the Uyghur migration was consequential beyond the movement itself.

The Karakhanid dynasty cannot be said to have been a strong, unified dynasty or power, politically or militarily. This dynasty had extreme historical significance, however, as it played the greatest role in the Turkification and Islamization of the western half of Central Asia.

The ultimate expression of this role was that the Karakhanids inspired the formation of the Seljuk dynasty. This event would later result in the overthrow of the Buwayhid dynasty and the rise of the sultans, and even led to the Crusades. We can say that the Karakhanid dynasty of the western half of Central Asia was the driving force of the political history of the ancient Near East in the eleventh century and beyond.

In terms of Turkification and Islamization, however, Sogdians and other peoples of Iranian descent were on the rise in Ma Wara al-Nahr (Transoxania)—the now-defunct Sogdiana. The ascent of these Islamized peoples was due to the grip they maintained on their commercial rights and the business community to their west, whose heart was the Islamic world.

This state of affairs began in the period of the Turkic khaganate, long before Islamization. The situation was similar to that of the eastern half of Central Asia, which was not Islamized. In short, a substratum of

Table. Islamization and Turkification of Central Asia as of the 11th Century

	Region	
	Western Half (West Turkistan)	Eastern Half (East Turkistan)
Polity	Karakhanid Dynasty	Uyghur Kingdom of Qocho
Status	Islamization with inconsistent Turkification	Turkification without Islamization
Settled Peoples	Muslims of **Iranian Descent** (Persian-speaking)	Uyghurs of **Sogdian Descent** (Turkic-speaking)
Ruling Classes	**Turkic Nomads** (Muslims)	**Turkic Nomads** (Non-Muslims)

Boldface highlights indicate people present in both eastern and western Central Asia.

merchants of Iranian origin and a superstratum of nomadic rulers who protected them formed the social organization.

This organizational structure existed in parallel, east and west across the Pamirs, irrespective of the presence or absence of Islam. The table shows the foregoing discussion in abstract terms.

In this structure, Turkic power was the superstratum, constituting a military and political might that was more closely related to the commerce and economy of the substratum, and which supported and protected the activities of that substratum. This phenomenon was most pronounced in Central Asia, through the long westward migration and settlement of the Uyghurs.

The phenomenon itself was not limited to "Turkified" Central Asia. It also occurred in East and West Asia, to varying degrees.

Turkic Supremacy and Climatic Warming

These movements that revolved around "Turkification" of Central Asia integrated parallel phenomena in East and West Asia. To the question of what caused these trends, no single answer will suffice. If asked to cite the single most fundamental, most universal cause, however, it would likely be the climatic warming that was finally becoming conspicuous at the time.

I have already described in Chapter One the great impact of global climatic cooling, which had become significant beginning in the third century. The grassland and oasis ecosystems of the Eurasian interior were damaged particularly severely. The shrinkage of the grasslands directly affected the fates of the peoples who lived there. Migrations of nomads seeking to survive became increasingly frequent, and the resulting cascade phenomenon plunged the agricultural lands into varying degrees of chaos.

Searches for order amid such chaos led to regimes that unified vast regions: Islam in the west and the Tang in the east. The migrations of the Turkic nomadic forces dissolved such unification east and west, all at the same time as the climatic warming was happening.

The grasslands stopped shrinking and began to recover and grow again. The scope for nomadic activity expanded as a result, and new migrations became increasingly active. And the Turkic peoples were at the forefront.

The Western exemplars of these migrations were the activities of the aforementioned mamluks, who were at the center of the various Western Asian Islamic dynasties, where they held the real military and political power. Eventually, even a power referred to as "the Mamluk dynasty" came into existence.

The nearest East Asian parallel to the mamluks would probably be the *fanzhen* dominions in China, specifically Zhongyuan. This historical phenomenon happened in the tenth century, between the fall of the Tang and the "Five Dynasties" in northern China or "Ten Kingdoms" in southern China. Beginning in the ninth century, Zhongyuan was effectively the domain of the *fanzhen*, which were militarist cliques that could be considered the descendants of the An Lushan army—military forces in the manner of the Turkic nomads. The Tang had long since been reduced to a regional polity holding only the area around Chang'an, its distinctive Hu-Han unification having been nearly completely lost.

Among these ruling militarists, a Turkic force, the Shatuo tribe, rose to prominence. It seized control of the Zhongyuan entity that succeeded the Tang in the early half of the tenth century. This Shatuo-based power also formed the basis of the military force of the Song dynasty. Following its founding in 960, the Song sustained itself for over three hundred years over its Bei (Northern) and Nan (Southern) periods. The Turkic powers showed in this way that they could not be overlooked in either East or West Asia.

The Rise of the Khitai

The main actor in East Asia, however, was not necessarily the Shatuo polity of Zhongyuan. If anything, the tendency of the Turkic forces was to gradually fade away from East Asia. At the very least, they achieved nothing like the enterprise of the mamluks to the west in the same period.

As exemplified by the Uyghurs, Turkic nomadic forces migrated from east to west. With a little thought, it is probably obvious that the eastern lands they left behind differed in aspect from the western lands they moved into. And an even newer force was beginning to emerge on the eastern Mongolian Plateau vacated by the Turkic peoples.

If climatic warming and the expansion of grasslands sparked the Turkic migrations, then the same would naturally hold true for other nomadic tribes. Nor would ascendancy, activity, or migration be limited to the Turkic peoples, especially in East Asia.

Following the long westward movement of the Uyghurs and the collapse of the Tang, the Khitai, led by Yelü Abaoji, conquered the Mongolian Plateau in the early tenth century. This was a Mongol tribe that suddenly emerged from the grasslands of the upper reaches of the Liao River. Although the name of Khitai is found in records dating long before this time, they became truly mighty beginning in the reign of Yelü Abaoji.

As the land of Zhongyuan, to their south, was in the anarchic throes of the Five Dynasties, the Khitai was indeed known in the world at the time as the preeminent power in East Asia. "Khitai" is the origin of two names for China: Cathay in English, and Китай (Kitai) in Russian.

This shows how outsized the presence of the Khitai was. In fact, Chinese history through the tenth century revolved around conflict between the Khitai and the Shatuo polity of the Five Dynasties, in which the latter was constantly overwhelmed. This state of affairs did not change noticeably even after the chaotic Five Dynasties period ended and the Northern Song dynasty began.

While the Yelü imperial bloodline of the Khitai was Mongol in nature, the Xiao clan, which produced many empresses, was said to be of Uyghur extraction, providing ties with the prior Turkic peoples. Such alliances and mergers between the Mongols and the Turkic peoples would provide the basic structure of the future nomadic grassland region. In all these ways, the Khitai state broke new ground in East Asia.

Even more remarkable, the group that controlled the Khitai comprised nomadic hunters, living a life of annual seasonal migration. At the same time, however, in nomadic grasslands belonging to emperors and their lords, the Khitai constructed walled cities, where it settled Han and other agricultural peoples, turning these cities into important hubs for food production.

The Uyghur, which had previously reigned over the Mongolian Plateau, was a nomadic state that had maintained walled cities. Later settlement in oasis cities by the westward-moving Uyghurs might be due to their experience of urban living.

City management by the Khitai might also have come from their strong relations with the Uyghur. It is also possible that these relations were connected to the Khitai devotion to Buddhism. These relations may additionally have been instrumental in the Khitai control of frontier regions between farming and herding, where the Han resided. These regions included the so-called "Sixteen Prefectures of Yan and Yun," which has become the present-day Beijing-Datong belt.

Thus, under the Khitai, the nomadic and agricultural spheres were bound together even more organically than before, and accordingly began preparing the ground for a single-state system.

The Tang-Song Transition

While the Khitai was growing in strength and overpowering the southern Zhongyuan state, it was fostering ever-closer relations with the agricultural spheres. In addition to claiming the Sixteen Prefectures of Yan and Yun, the Khitai destroyed the Shatuo state of the Five Dynasties in 947. Settling down in the Huang He Basin, the Khitai even attempted to govern Zhongyuan directly. It was at this time that it adopted "Liao" as the Chinese-style dynasty name of its state. The attempt ended in failure, and the Khitai retreated northward. It did not abandon its commitment to Zhongyuan, however. Its show of interest in the region was probably because it was drawn to the region's economic power.

In the academic community of Chinese historical studies, the period beginning before the tenth century and ending sometime thereafter is typically referred to as the time of the Tang-Song transition. The idea was advocated by the aforementioned Naito Konan, a Japanese trailblazer of Eastern historical studies. It signifies that Chinese civilization in the tenth century and later, under the Song, has a completely different aspect than that in the ninth century and earlier, under the Tang. It has become axiomatic nearly the world over.

This reformation extended to all areas, from politics to culture. It is possible that the influx of Iranian culture and the adoption of the advanced civilization of the western ancient Near East, both prominent in the Tang period, had a significant effect. Climatic warming might have also been a factor.

Here, I propose to elucidate the increased production and economic development within China, as well as the technological innovations that made these possible. This includes farm production, of course, as well as the work of preparing cropland. Nor can we overlook the increased production of the metals that would become the tools for these activities. That increased production would be the force driving all these efforts.

But increasing the manufacture of metals and ironware requires immense amounts of heat energy. And the use of coal for fuel was becoming common practice in China at the time. Indeed, China was in the very midst of an energy revolution.

There is no doubt that this economic development on the part of China and the growing power and prosperity of the Khitai or East Asian nomadic forces were strongly interrelated at the root. Metal and ironware can be made into weapons as well as tools. And when the manufacture of such implements increased, China could not possibly keep them all for itself. They leaked outward, strengthening the military forces at China's periphery. The armed forces of the agricultural areas, which depended on infantry, found it even more difficult to oppose the superiority of nomadic states' cavalries.

Even so, there was not an exact congruence between politics and the military. Nomadic forces might have had sufficient knowledge to govern cities in less expansive regions. However, the know-how for governing the totality of a vast agricultural region had still not been established, not without the nomadic forces breaking up their own group organization. The Khitai had been trying and failing to do so for a long time. Although it far surpassed the Zhongyuan state in military might, the Khitai never succeeded in building an order capable of ruling the whole of East Asia.

Systems of Multipartite Coexistence

Stability came for a time with the founding of the Song dynasty. The Northern Song, which integrated Zhongyan in the Huang He Basin and Jiangnan in the Chang Jiang Basin, established rule by monarchical autocracy, stabilizing the political situation and authority south of the Great Wall.

Thus, a force was at last established that was capable of contending with the Khitai. Although the Northern Song was no military match for the Khitai, it had an overwhelming advantage in economic and material terms. With such leverage, it became possible for the Khitai and the Northern Song to establish a system whereby both parties could coexist in mutual prosperity.

The Khitai and the Northern Song made a pact, establishing diplomatic ties in a relationship of functional equals. The pact was known as the Treaty of Chanyuan. In exchange for making an annual gift of a colossal amount of wealth to the Khitai, the safety of the Northern Song's northern frontier was guaranteed, allowing them to celebrate peace. This was in the year 1004. This relationship, beginning with the dawn of the eleventh century—and entangling other countries as well—lasted for some two hundred years, until the advent of Genghis Khan and the Mongol Empire.

This does not mean, of course, that there were no complications. In modern terms, the relation of equals between the Khitai and the Northern Song would be called a balance of power, and the stability of both was a necessary condition for that balance. And that stability experienced a jolt roughly a century after the conclusion of the Treaty of Chanyuan. The Tungusic Jurchens, who lived in forests to the east of the Khitai, abruptly grew in strength and wiped out both the Khitai and the Northern Song.

However, the growth of the Jurchens' might was much too sudden. Although the Jin dynasty founded by the Jurchens moved southward,

I. Central and East Asia in the 11th Century

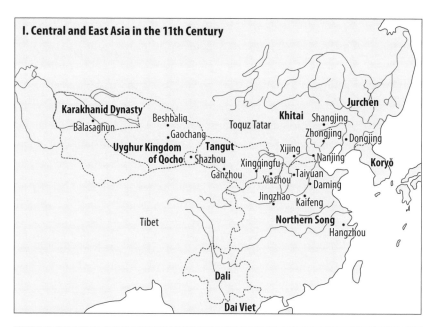

II. Central and East Asia in the 12th Century

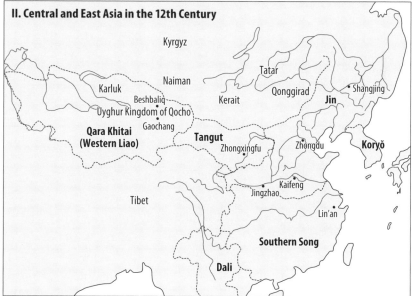

Fig. 16. Multipartite Coexistent Structures

conquering and subjugating the Huang He Plains, the dynasty's strength did not extend as far as Jiangnan. The Jin permitted the existence of the Southern Song dynasty, and the two made a new pact, rebuilding a system of coexistence.

Such a system of coexistence was unusual in East Asian history. The norm had been one where power imbalances became significant and the superior hegemon subjugated the peoples in its vicinity. Even close-matched forces did not necessarily lead to long-term peace.

With this in mind, we can view the peaceful coexistence of this period as groundbreaking. The nomadic force's military might and prosperity and the agricultural region's economic progress were both interrelated and in unyielding confrontation. One could describe it as a system of order that emerged atop this balance. Conversely, when the balance was upset, a new stage—a new period—in history began.

Prerequisites for the Rise of the Mongol Empire

The might of the Jurchen failed to expand in directions other than just to their south. They were also unable to establish control west of the Mongolian Plateau. The remnants of the Northern Song fled southward, reconstituting themselves as the Southern Song. Similarly, the remnants of the Khitai fled westward and reconstituted their regime. Yelü Dashi, a member of the Liao imperial family, leading the clan forces under his banner, conquered both the Uyghur kingdom of Qocho and the Karakhanid dynasty in Central Asia. This polity was known in Chinese as the Western Liao, which the local inhabitants called Qara Khitai in Persian. Yelü Dashi aspired to further restore formerly held lands, and even attempted an eastward campaign in this regard. He was ultimately unsuccessful, however.

Whatever Yelü Dashi's plans may have been, the Khitai western campaign closely resembled the long westward movement of the Turkic Uyghurs, and marked in its turn the beginning of a long westward movement of Mongols. Seen from this viewpoint, the emergence of Qara Khitai was historically significant in at least two ways, both of which became prerequisites for the future founding of the Mongol Empire.

Firstly, Qara Khitai unified the Turkified eastern and western parts of Central Asia. The long westward movement of the Turkic peoples and the Turkification of the great oasis belt had never achieved the unification of the region. The Mongol nomadic forces, consisting of the Khitai, succeeded where these earlier efforts had failed. And roughly a century later, the cavalry of the Mongol Empire would repeat this accomplishment on an even grander scale.

Secondly, owing to the lack of success of the eastern campaign by Qara Khitai, the Mongolian Plateau underwent repeated breakups and conflicts between various warlords, with no strong power taking hold and establishing rule and control there. Thus, a situation developed in which tribes without a common leader vied with each other, playing out life-or-death struggles. From this crucible of conflict, Genghis and his armies emerged.

CHAPTER 3

THE FORMATION OF
EARLY MODERN ASIA

1. Building the Mongol Empire

The Advent of the Mongols

In previous chapters, I have used the place name "Mongolian Plateau" without providing any explanation for doing so. Properly speaking, however, this region came to be called "Mongolia" after the historical emergence of the Mongols and the buildup of their resolute forces. The name has been nothing more than a convenient placeholder thus far in this book.

We now approach the period when it will be appropriate in name and fact to call this area the "Mongolian Plateau." With the emergence of Genghis Khan (c. 1162–1227) on the world stage, tribes that had been in gruesome conflict with one another would follow him as a federation. This state-like confederation of the Mongols, or Yeke Mongol Uls (the Great Mongol Uls), would thus be inaugurated at the start of the thirteenth century. (Note: *Uls* is a romanization of a Mongolian word originally meaning tribe or people; it pertains less to land or territory than to a grouping of persons. Though it roughly equates to state, it remains a political construct specific to Mongolian society.)

The building of the Mongol Empire began with Genghis and reached its zenith with his grandson Khubilai. That empire's conquest of Eurasia is a highly dramatic and famous chapter of history expounded endlessly by well-known scholars in years gone by. There is no need for an outsider to venture to recite it in detail. Let us just establish the outline and the essential points.

Asian history through the twelfth century was made up of periods of confrontation and coexistence in eastern as well as western regions. The situation was one in which forces north and south were multipolarized, on a par with each other, and antagonistic.

The nomads' activities, which had become ever more animated due to the climatic warming that began in the previous century, led to a new phase that arose as they reconstituted their forces everywhere. The Tang-Song transition—the technological revolution in East Asia—also had a significant impact on this development.

Among the evenly matched elements that brought about this multipolarization

Genghis Khan (Yuan Taizu)
Photo courtesy of National Palace Museum, Taipei. (https://theme.npm.edu.tw/opendata/)

were force of arms, economies, and cultures. As no clear superiority could be easily discerned, various regimes were able to coexist as separate entities. Thus, if it so happened that one regime should gain an edge and disrupt the existing balance, the positions of all the regimes concerned would shift accordingly. The advent of the Mongols in the thirteenth century can be thought of as just such an event.

Genghis and his followers, the so-called Great Mongol Uls, emerged as a nomadic force superior to anyone in military might. The process of restructuring Eurasia began with this disruption in the military balance.

The Conquest of the Eastern and Western Steppes

In the 1210s, the first opponent whom the Mongols challenged head-on, soon after their inception, was the Jin dynasty, situated on the Mongols' eastern flank. Despite asserting that it was merely an observer of events, the Jin was the master manipulator that caused various forces to oppose one another on the Mongolian Plateau, making the region a site for conflict. It could be said to be an archenemy of Genghis and the Mongol armies.

Accordingly, the utmost objective of the war was Mongol independence, and the Mongols invested practically all of their forces in the fighting. Genghis thereby achieved victory, dealing the Jin a great blow.

He conquered the steppe belt north of what is now Beijing, absorbed the nomadic warriors formerly of the Khitai, and rose to become the supreme power in East Asia. The Mongols, further increasing in military might, then turned westward.

The situation to their west was one step ahead of the east in multi-polarization and balance of power, beginning with the Turkification of Central Asia. Thus, that balance had been experiencing failures for a long time. And the epicenter was, again, Central Asia.

Qara Khitai, which had integrated the entire area, was by this time already collapsing. The Naiman tribe, having been chased from the Mongolian Plateau by Genghis, had wrested control of Qara Khitai in 1212. That being the case in the eastern half of Central Asia, the Khwarezm-Shah dynasty in the western half achieved independence and extended its might over the land like the rays of the morning sun.

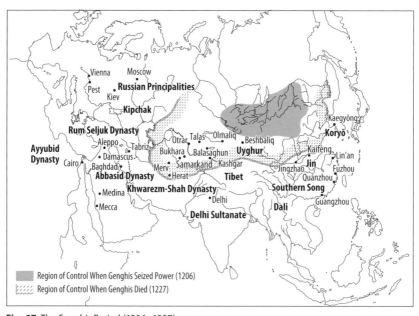

Fig. 17. The Genghis Period (1206–1227)
Adapted from Honda Minobu, *Mongoru jidaishi kenkyu* [Historical Studies on the Mongol Domination] (Tokyo: University of Tokyo Press, 1991), Appendix 2.

The Khwarezm-Shah dynasty started out as a Turkic nomadic force that rose to power in the latter half of the eleventh century in the Khwarezm area along the lower reaches of the Amu River. At the start of the thirteenth century, the Khwarezm-Shahs allied with the Naiman, broke the ties that bound them to Qara Khitai, swept over Ma Wara al-Nahr (Transoxania) and the Iranian Plateau, and generally gloried in their might as though they dominated the whole of Western Asia.

The amazing expansion of the Khwarezm-Shahs happened at the same time as the rise to power of the Mongols far to their east. Was it coincidence or a rising tendency toward integration? Whatever the case, the situation was such that a collision between dramatically growing eastern and western powers was inevitable.

In 1218, the Mongols overthrew the Naimans who had seized power from Qara Khitai, thereby moving into Central Asia. Beginning the following year, they moved west, carrying out a campaign against the Khwarezm-Shahs, and in just over a year, controlled Ma Wara al-Nahr (Transoxania). Unable, however, to expand their power across the Amu River to Khorasan, in 1222 the Mongols turned their horses around.

The eventful life of Genghis came to an end five years later. By that point, the Mongols expanded to a scale of power encompassing the eastern and western grassland and oasis regions. As for what this meant in historical terms, finding an answer would have to wait for a later time.

Regime Systemization

At heart, the Mongols led by Genghis could be said to be almost entirely a nomadic military band. In that sense, they were only unsophisticated, sincere warriors, "unadorned and undistracted," to paraphrase later Han Chinese writings. In the time of the extraordinary hero Genghis—who triumphed in war, built a country, and lived almost entirely for military action—that was probably good enough.

It would not do, however, after his demise in 1227. Having grown into a polity bringing together diverse peoples in a vast space, the Great Mongol Uls needed a harmonious administration. To that end, it needed support from people who had the know-how to manage preexisting organizations in situ. The now-defunct Khitai served as an immediate model, and their alumni participated in the administration of the Mongol domain from the outset.

At the time, the Mongols, having accomplished this expansion, controlled the whole of the former Khitai region, including Qara Khitai. This was true both spatially and structurally. In other words, the Mongol nomads of the eastern grassland belt subdued the western Turkic nomads and entered into collaborations with the settled peoples of Iranian and Turkic descent in the oasis areas.

The enterprise of Genghis, who conquered the eastern and western grassland and oasis regions, meant unification of the Mongolian Plateau with Central Asia, which the now-defunct Khitai had failed to accomplish. Nor was that all. An even more solid unification was achieved between the Mongol-Turkic armed forces and the Turkic-Iranian economic powers living in the region. This unification would become clear for all to see in the political management of the period to come.

Genghis was succeeded by his third son, Ögödei (c. 1186–1241), who was considered a consensus choice. The systemization of the regime was an urgent concern for both Ögödei and the Mongol people. The greatest exponents of this effort were the construction of Karakorum, the capital of the steppes, and the devising thereafter of *jamchi*, a network of postal relay stations. These stations facilitated communications, the supply of food and horses, and taxation.

Karakorum was founded in reaction to assaults on castle towns operated by such predecessor nomadic states as the Uyghur and the Khitai. It was also a clear expression that the Mongols were the successor to those political entities. Khitans

Ögödei (Yuan Taizong)
Photo courtesy of National Palace Museum, Taipei. (https://theme.npm.edu.tw/opendata/)

and Uyghurs, who handled taxation and record-keeping, instituted and carried out the business of government under the rulership of Ögödei.

In less than thirty years, the Mongols had conquered a large portion of the expansive grassland and oasis regions, and thus faced the prospect of the various lands being balkanized without a scheme to bind strategic points together. Creating a network of postal relay stations with Karakorum at its center was therefore essential. It made for unbroken communication with the influential people controlling those strategic points as well as with frontline armies. The ruler was thus able to transmit directives, asserting his command over the whole of his lands without his having to move from the center.

East-West Expansion

Newly in charge, the Mongols needed to implement an even greater show of military strength and expanded force in order to preserve the influence and power established in the Genghis period. They thus embarked on campaigns to their east and west. To the east, the plan was to annihilate the Jin, who by this time were reduced to cowering in the Zhongyuan Huang He Basin. After five years of heavy fighting, the Jin dynasty fell in 1234, and the Mongols were able to flaunt their status as the preeminent force in East Asia.

At this point, the Mongols made a concerted effort to control Zhongyuan, further strengthening their relations and conflicts with China. In 1236, they sent an expeditionary force to the Southern Song, who had an uneasy coexistence with the Jin to their south. The attempted campaign failed in its early stages, however, leading to a postponement in the Mongol showdown with the Southern Song.

Of even more concern at the time was the westward campaign begun the same year. The northwestern conquest, which Genghis had entrusted to his eldest son, Jochi, was aborted due to Jochi's death. It thus fell to Jochi's son Batu to carry out this campaign from scratch.

Batu's Mongol forces began by entering the great steppe belt north of the Caspian Sea, the Caucasus, and the Black Sea. They subjugated the

Kipchaks, who had deep roots in the region. The name "Kipchak" was a general label for nomadic bands of Turkic descent. Batu's army, having absorbed the Kipchaks, was unmatched in strength or aggression and advanced farther west, into Russia, in 1237. The whole of Russia, where numerous principalities struggled with one another, fell under Mongol control without hope of resistance. This marks the historical start of the assemblage known as Russia.

Batu's western expeditionary force moved even farther west, sweeping over eastern Europe and defeating the armies of Poland, the Teutonic Order, and Hungary. If not for the demise of Ögödei late in 1241, who maintained the heart of the Mongol *uls* on the Mongolian Plateau, and the remand notice that ordered Batu to return to the Mongol homeland on the occasion of the Great Khan's death, he might well have penetrated as far as Western Europe.

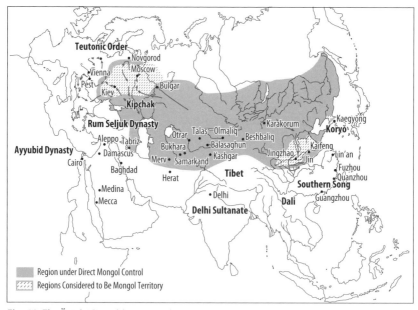

Fig. 18. The Ögödei Period (1229–1241)
Adapted from Honda Minobu, *Mongoru jidaishi kenkyu* [Historical Studies on the Mongol Domination] (Tokyo: University of Tokyo Press, 1991), Appendix 2.

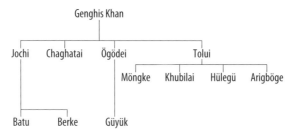

Fig. 19. Simplified Genghis Genealogy

Though Batu did not advance farther than this point, North Asia thus at last emerged as one of history's staging areas (see Fig. 4, Area III, p. 39). Prior to this time, there were practically no facts sufficient to be called either history or Asian history. Thereafter, under Mongol control, history would progress to a point which would lead to the first stirrings of the Russian Empire.

Russians and Westerners alike would call this empire the Tatar Yoke. We might consider this label yet another instance of Eurocentrism.

The Second Stage

At this point, the expansion of the Mongol Empire paused temporarily. An interval of some ten years would elapse. During that time, there was a family feud over succession, and control passed from the house of Ögödei to the line of Ögödei's youngest brother, Tolui. Upon his election as Great Khan in 1251, Möngke, Tolui's eldest son (1208–1259), promptly suppressed his opponents, strengthened his power base, and then devised and carried out a new plan of campaign.

In some fifty years after Genghis' beginnings, the Mongols had succeeded in conquering the grassland and oasis regions. After taking control of the Mongolian Plateau, Genghis united Central Asia. This represented the union of the core territory of the nomadic areas. His successor, Ögödei, further expanded the Mongol domains to Zhongyuan

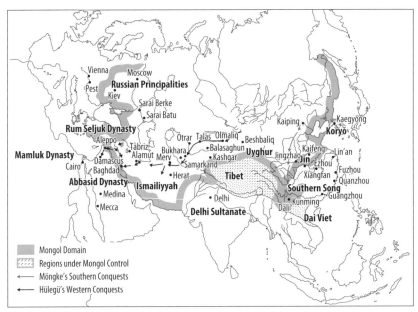

Fig. 20. The Möngke Period (1251–1259)
Adapted from Honda Minobu, *Mongoru jidaishi kenkyu* [Historical Studies on the Mongol Domination] (Tokyo: University of Tokyo Press, 1991), Appendix 2.

and the Kipchak Steppe to the southeast and northwest of the Mongolian Plateau. These were either grassland regions, or else they were arid zones where nomads and farmers met and mingled. We might call this enterprise the integration of the entire Central Eurasian region. The scale of the endeavor was greater than anything attempted since the time of the Turkic khaganate.

The endeavor meant that this region, containing the entirety of the arid zone that spans Areas I, II, III, and IV in Figure 4 (p. 39), was under the sole command of the Mongols. It was thus possible to deploy into the agricultural lands on the region's periphery. And the Mongol expansion in the latter half of the thirteenth century, under Möngke and his successors, was devised with just this design in mind.

Möngke commanded Khubilai (1215–1294), the second of Tolui's four sons, to attack to the east, and ordered Hülegü (1218–1265), third of the four, to attack to the west. The former's target was Jiangnan—China south of the Huai River—while the latter concentrated on the Iran *zamin* (Iranian lands) west of the Amu River. Each of these was a densely populated land where agriculture was predominant and whose people took pride in civilizations dating back to ancient times. And Mongol power had not extended to either one.

The conquests of both would complete the unification of the Asian world—the whole of Eurasia, not just its "central" portion—a world which had undergone repeated multipolarization, north-south hostility, and conflict in the previous century. It seems clear that this was Möngke's goal. It would be appropriate to call this the second stage of the Mongol Empire.

Hülegü's Western Conquests

Having been entrusted with overall command of the western expeditionary force, Hülegü set out from the Mongolian Plateau in 1253. Over the next two years, he built up a large army as he advanced over Central Asia, mustering troop strength at every stop along the way.

It was near the end of 1255 when, quietly bringing pressure to bear on his periphery with a slow-moving march, Hülegü reached the bank of the Amu River. Once there, he interrogated the various forces of the Iran *zamin* to determine whether they would oppose him. Discerning that most of them would not, Hülegü crossed the Amu and advanced his army soon after the start of the following year. The army's marching speed had made a sudden change from slow to fast.

The first target attacked by Hülegü's army was the Ismailites, one of the most radical breakaway sects of Shia Islam and the founders of the Fatimid dynasty. Led in the eleventh century by Hasan-e Sabbah (d. 1124), the order extended its power to the Iranian Plateau. It was very hostile to the Seljuk dynasty, who were believers in the primacy of Sunnah, the orthodox teachings of Muhammad. It is said that the Ismaili use of tactics of murder by infiltration against their enemies gave rise to their being called "assassins."

From a mountain base centered on the hill fortress of Alamut, the Ismailites established an independent regime, building a vast sphere of influence reaching as far south as Fars and as far east as Khorasan. In any event, there was no military force in the Iran *zamin* superior to the Ismailites. Thus, it was only natural that the Mongols should target them first.

Upon being attacked, however, the head of the Ismailites promptly surrendered. Alamut, the fortress that had been their stronghold, capitulated without resistance, submitting to the Mongol army with practically no combat to speak of. By late 1256, opposition by all worthy enemy forces thus ceased—less than a year after Hülegü crossed the Amu.

Next, Hülegü wasted no time in deploying his army toward Iraq. His second target was the Abbasid dynasty. Although they had long since lost the might with which they had long ago conquered the entirety of the ancient Near East, the Abbasids nonetheless retained tremendous authority among Muslims in the person of the Sunni caliphs. Thus, they represented a possible obstacle to the Mongol plans of conquest.

Hülegü encircled Baghdad, capital of the Abbasid dynasty, with watertight positions. Early in 1258, he captured the caliph al-Musta'sim and put him to death. By February of that year, the Abbasid dynasty fell, after some five hundred years of rule. The caliphs were also no more. And having suddenly lost both its radical Shia and its orthodox Sunni sects, which constituted the core of the Islamic sphere, Islam itself was forced into a new era.

This was, of course, by no means the end of Hülegü's western conquests. From Iraq he moved his army to Syria, bringing about the surrender of Aleppo in February 1260 and of Damascus the following April. Truly, no one could withstand his onslaught.

Having brought Syria under his control, he would logically have turned his attentions to Anatolia, Egypt, and the Mediterranean, which now lay before him. By conquering these regions, Hülegü might well have aspired to reunite the ancient Near East as the Achaemenid, Umayyad, and Abbasid dynasties had done before him. Such ambitions, however, would go unfulfilled.

As he was forming ranks at Aleppo, just after its surrender, Hülegü resolved to return eastward with his main force, for he had received word of the death of his eldest brother, Möngke, the Great Khan.

Khubilai's Usurpation

At the time, Möngke was encamped in Sichuan. As to what he, commander-in-chief of the Mongols, was doing personally leading a campaign when he should have been in his home base of the Mongolian Plateau, that is where this story begins.

Möngke had entrusted the conquest and rule of China to his younger brother Khubilai. Khubilai had, however, avoided a frontal assault on the Southern Song in Jiangnan. Instead, in 1253 he went out of his way to the west and, after capturing only Yunnan, prepared for a prolonged conflict. He knew how difficult that assault would be. In the process, however, Khubilai incurred the wrath of the Great Khan Möngke, who had desired a decisive offensive leading to a quick settlement.

In 1258, Möngke led his own army on campaign against Sichuan, and pressing on Khubilai, ordered him to gain control of the middle reaches of Chang Jiang. Before Khubilai could mobilize his forces, however, Möngke sent his main force into battle first, where it promptly fell into a stalemate. In the course of these events, Möngke died an untimely death in the summer of 1259 from an epidemic that was rampant at the time.

Without a Great Khan, both the Mongolian homeland and the Chinese front were bound to fall into chaos. Arigböge (1219–1266), fourth and youngest of Tolui's sons, whom Möngke had left in charge of the homeland, attempted to continue Möngke's regime as a matter of course. Eventually, after official procedure was followed, Arigböge was named Great Khan.

Conversely, Khubilai, fighting on other fronts, was still smarting from Möngke's reprimand. Even if he were to obey the new ruler, he would be certain to find himself at a disadvantage, given that that new ruler was adopting Möngke's line. Instead, Khubilai gathered his army, which was scattered throughout southern China, and returned northward. With this large military force at his command, Khubilai independently acceded to the rank of Great Khan, at Kaiping. This was in 1260. Kaiping was a castle town that Khubilai had constructed four years earlier, on the grasslands at the southeastern corner of the Mongolian Plateau. It had served as his stronghold for the subjugation of China.

Khubilai, Founder of the Dai-ön Yeke Mongol Uls (Yuan Dynasty)
Photo from History/Bridgeman Images

The resulting situation was one of two giants, evenly matched—neither of whom would concede. In the final analysis, the difference in military might was the deciding factor. Though he may have lacked legitimacy, Khubilai, with superior arms, overwhelmed his opponent's forces. In 1264, Arigböge surrendered, and the new administration of Khubilai was inaugurated in fact as well as in name.

At this time, the house of Batu, who was governing the northwest as far as Russia; Hülegü, who was fighting numerous battles in West Asia; and the house of Chaghatai, in Central Asia, all maintained their respective forces. Chaghatai (d. 1242), second son of Genghis, had based his clan in the Ili Valley, near Olmaliq. For the sake of survival, all of these factions had no choice but to recognize Khubilai's hegemonic rule in East Asia. The house of Chaghatai had especially suffered oppression on the occasion of Möngke's accession as Great Khan and declined as a result. Thus, it enthusiastically aligned itself with Khubilai's usurpation and plotted the restoration of its prestige. This was when the framework of the Mongol Empire that dominated Eurasia took shape.

2. The Achievements of the Mongols

Expansion Halted

The exterior shape of the Mongol Empire was essentially complete when Khubilai ascended as Great Khan in 1264. Thereafter, the rule of Khubilai, which is to say the Dai-ön Yeke Mongol Uls (Dai-ön Uls; i.e., the Yuan dynasty), engaged in a campaign of conquest to annex the Southern Song. However, the explosive armed Mongol expansion that had spanned the first half of the thirteenth century at last came to a halt. One could say that having reached the limits of its growth, the Mongol Empire left the founding and establishment phase and entered that of preservation and maintenance.

The catalyst for this transition was the course of action taken by Hülegü, third of the four sons of Tolui, who was in the process of his western conquests. Upon receiving the news of the death of his eldest brother, Möngke, in 1260, Hülegü promptly turned his army back, in hopes of becoming the next Great Khan.

By the time Hülegü returned to Tabriz in Azerbaijan, however, news reached him that Khubilai, his second eldest brother, had established himself as ruler of his own *uls*. Hülegü realized that Khubilai would be fighting with Arigböge, their youngest brother, who was located in the heartland of Mongolia. Accordingly, Hülegü established his own independent domain where he was at the time, so as to observe the developing situation between his siblings. History records this event as the founding of the Hülegü Uls.

Prior to these actions, in the spring of that year Hülegü had left a cavalry vanguard numbering slightly more than ten thousand in Syria, on the occasion of his turning back from Aleppo. This residual Mongol force advanced on Egypt, where it met resistance from the Mamluk dynasty. The Mongols were routed on September 2, 1260, at the Battle of Ayn Jalut.

The defeated Mongol army had no choice but to withdraw from Syria. The Mamluk dynasty thus avoided a crisis, secured Syria, and maintained a standoff with the Mongols. The reach of Hülegü's forces would thereafter form the boundaries of Iran. This situation represented a clean break with the Arab world from Syria westward, which was ruled by the Mamluk dynasty. In this moment, the structure of the Islamic world was decided. That structure remains in place to this day.

Having been blocked from moving farther west, Hülegü's forces found relations strained to their north as well. Hülegü's western conquests had originally been conducted by the Mongols en masse in the Möngke period. Hence, the expeditionary forces involved did not belong to Hülegü alone: they had been formed of nomads recruited in Mongolia, Central Asia, and the northwest Kipchak Steppe. It was inevitable that these other forces and regions should think it unjust that their battles should result in Hülegü's independence. The Jochi Uls of the House of Batu found the grasslands of Azerbaijan to their south particularly

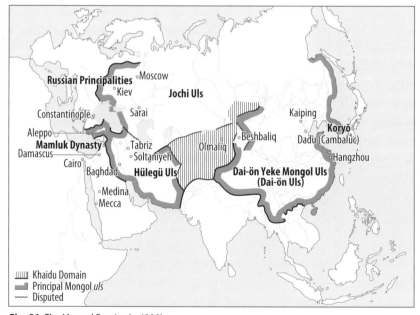

Fig. 21. The Mongol Empire (c. 1300)
Adapted from Honda Minobu, *Mongoru jidaishi kenkyu* [Historical Studies on the Mongol Domination] (Tokyo: University of Tokyo Press, 1991), Appendix 2.

appetizing. Consequently, they were fierce enemies of the Hülegü Uls, which was headquartered in Tabriz.

Thus, the independent formation of the Hülegü Uls stirred up conflict among the Mongols themselves, making their further outward growth impossible. Hülegü's untimely death soon after he declared the founding of his own *uls* made the West Asian political situation even more uncertain. There was also instability in Central Asia, due to strife between the House of Chaghatai and the House of Ögödei. Large-scale hostilities broke out with the Hülegü Uls. As with the internal Mongol confrontations, this was another conflict—this time across the Amu River—with no easy resolution. All of these factions had variously shifting allegiances with Khubilai's Dai-ön Uls in East Asia. The ongoing situation seemed likely to descend into internecine conflict (see Fig. 21).

With outward expansion no longer an option, the course of all the Mongols had to change. Khubilai, now elected Great Khan, would set that course.

The Summation of the Nomadic Regimes

From the vantage point of later times, we can evaluate the unification of Eurasia under the Mongol Empire as the summation of developments in Asian and world history to that point: to wit, the coexistence, competition, and progress among nomadism, farming, and commerce. The Mongol Empire unified Eurasia, prepared the ground for the period to come, flung open the door to that coming period, and then vanished. And such an evaluation would hold true everywhere, not only in East and West Asia but also in Japan and Europe. The course of Asian history was set for a time as well, by way of the hundred years of the rise and decline of the Mongol Empire in the fourteenth century. And the countenance of world history would be very different after this time.

We know this because more extensive archives survive from the Mongol unification of Eurasia than from any prior time. Okada Hidehiro (1931–2017), a professor of Eastern history, named this circumstance "the birth of world history" (Okada, *Sekaishi no tanjo: Mongoru no hatten to dento*

[The Birth of World History: Mongol Advancement and Tradition]). These materials further clarify the historical developments in all parts of Asia.

The expansion of Mongol power in the first half of the thirteenth century was the unification by Genghis and Ögödei of the grassland and oasis regions—that is, Central Eurasia. Other nomadic regimes that ruled this region include such predecessors of the Mongols as the Khwarezm-Shah dynasty, Qara Khitai, and the Kingdom of Qocho. In particular, of regimes that based themselves on the Mongolian Plateau, there was the Khitai, which preceded Qara Khitai. The Uyghur and Turkic khaganates had their day even farther back in time.

Conditions did not change much over time, whether natural and ecological or social and occupational. Their specific elements were the following: deserts and other arid zones; the nomads in those regions who sought grasslands; the settled peoples living and farming in the oases scattered across those arid zones; and the commerce that took place where nomads and settled peoples met.

Polities founded by nomadic forces under these conditions frequently consisted of dominions over vast areas. Like the oceans, the deserts and grasslands included in these nomadic domains were mostly empty of resident populations. Thus, the nomads could communicate rapidly over long distances, albeit with some degree of risk.

Horses made traversing long distances across the steppes easy and quick, much as ships could cross bodies of water from one coast to another at a single stretch. In this sense, the wide spaces of the nomadic regimes were comparable to later maritime states such as the British Empire.

However large these nomadic domains were, they varied in breadth and stability depending on circumstances. Each of these polities had their own answers to the question of how to form and stabilize relations between nomads and settled peoples.

Nomadic forces had overwhelming military superiority. Thus, it stood to reason that they would rule. Settled societies, however, had economic power and larger populations. How did these nomadic regimes connect, assemble, and systematize the military authority of the former and the private economy of the latter? The question of historical interest is how reliable and sustainable were the solutions that these entities found.

We find indications of trial and error dating back to the era of the Turkic khaganate. And like processes happened over and over in all of these nomadic regimes. In the Mongol Empire, the relations between nomadic and settled peoples at last attained an established shape.

War and Trade

Differences in ecosystems and customs between nomads and settled people frequently had to be compensated for. Solutions were arrived at in times of crisis by pillage or war. Such situations, however, were the exception. In most peacetime situations, nomads and settled peoples established relations through trade and negotiation.

Both parties were functionally integrated based on such trade and negotiation. The private-sector economy and the military might of the nomads were interdependent and complementary. The former provided resources to the latter, and the latter protected the former.

Such interrelations fit the prototype discussed previously in this book. And they developed along the so-called Silk Road. On the boundaries between the nomadic and agricultural regions, markets and cities emerged, and commerce and civilization progressed.

This commerce was specifically conducted via caravan. The resulting long-range economic relations had long been the sole province of the Sogdian merchants. They accordingly held sway in international economics. Their extensive economic influence and bargaining power helped propagate Persian civilization. Eventually the Sogdians linked up with Turkic and Tang military and political power to wield tremendous influence in East Asia. These developments are also discussed elsewhere in this book.

Before long, Central Asia, which had been the home base of the Sogdian merchants, would experience Turkification and Islamization. New groups would thereafter run the economy of Central Asia, across both the nomadic and settled spheres. These were Uyghur merchants of Sogdian descent in the east and Muslim merchants of Iranian descent in the west. The Pamirs became the overall east-west boundary between them.

The Khitai gained great power by allying itself with the Uyghur merchants of Sogdian descent. And it can be verified that the Muslim merchants of Iranian descent contributed to the increased might of the Khwarezm-Shah dynasty sometime after the Khitai. This latter development occurred on the eve of the Mongols' rise.

With these points in mind, while the initial growth of the Mongols under Genghis may have been simply an exercise in military conquest, its meaning went beyond that. The Mongols in this period allied with and co-opted the international big business centers of the time. And the Mongols would use them as a stepping stone to achieve even greater expansion.

The neighboring Uyghur kingdom of Qocho was the first to support the Mongols. Sugiyama Masaaki (b. 1952), a historian specializing in Central Eurasia and the Mongol period, describes the Uyghurs as "a brain trust of international scope." According to Sugiyama, these Uyghurs would "combine with the Mongols" to command the center of Mongol operations, to the extent that the Uyghurs "could even be said to be leading the Mongols and, in a sense, to have taken them over" (Sugiyama, *Yubokumin kara mita sekaishi*). That being so, the significance of this early allegiance given to the Mongols by the Uyghurs can hardly be overstated.

From there, Genghis headed west into Ma Wara al-Nahr (Transoxania). There, he overthrew the Khwarezm-Shah dynasty, and many of the Muslims of Iranian descent who had been ruled by that dynasty bowed down to the Mongols instead. The economic sphere that had been divided into east and west was thus unified under a single political entity. And the Silk Road, the largest artery in Eurasia, passed through that entire region.

Thus, the Uyghur merchants of Sogdian descent and the Muslim merchants of Iranian descent together were able to expand their trading regions east and west, and to make even greater profits. It would be no exaggeration to state that these merchant groups planned, promoted, and took advantage of the military and political growth of the Mongols.

There was, however, a mutual dependence in this arrangement. For their part, the Mongols had at their disposal the information and financial and negotiating resources afforded by the capital of the merchants. Thus, they were able to use these advantages to smoothly achieve their own political objectives.

Constructing a Metropolitan Region

The period of Mongol military expansion thus took the form of the nomads and the settled peoples allocating roles in a complementary manner, drawing on their respective strengths. Further military expansion had become difficult by Khubilai's time, however, and these methods would no longer serve. Economic prosperity was needed, of a kind which both the nomads and the settled peoples could enjoy, as appropriate to a period of preservation.

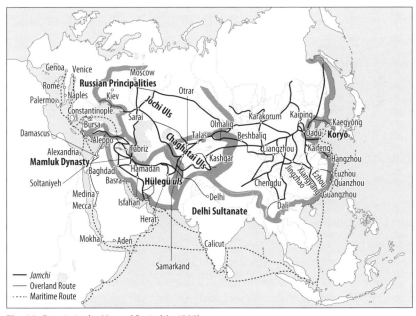

Fig. 22. Eurasia in the Mongol Period (c. 1300)
Adapted from Honda Minobu, *Mongoru jidaishi kenkyu* [Historical Studies on the Mongol Domination] (Tokyo: University of Tokyo Press, 1991), Appendix 2.

Khubilai demonstrated unparalleled ability in creating and managing an organization suited to this purpose. We could call the task he undertook following his ascension the building of just such a new system. This work included annexing Jiangnan, the heart of the Southern Song, which had the greatest population density of the time, as well as a high level of productivity.

The most visible aspect of Khubilai's works was the building of castle towns. Everyone knows that the present capital of China is Beijing. While the modern city stands in nearly the same location as such ancient predecessors as Yan and Youzhou, it nevertheless can only be traced back directly to the era of the Dai-ön Uls, and in particular to the latter half of the thirteenth century, after Khubilai seized power. To be sure, Beijing is a castle town founded originally by the Mongol ruler Khubilai.

The Beijing region is located at the northern edge of Zhongyuan, making it a border zone between farmers and nomads. This region would also mark the northern boundary of the agricultural region, as the Great Wall is just to its north. Kaiping, a strategically located castle town that Khubilai managed prior to this time, is located to the north of the Great Wall. It represents nearly the southernmost extent of the nomadic region. Upon taking control, Khubilai followed up Kaiping by constructing an even larger castle town where Beijing stands today. This was Dadu, also known in the West as Cambaluc.

The nomadic life involves annual migrations between summer and winter quarters. This remained true even after the nomads amassed great power and political machinery: they did not typically reside in cities. Their residences were tents known as *ordo* in Turkic and Mongol. As described previously, however, the Uyghur and Khitai constructed citadels in the midst of nomadic lands. They had settled peoples move to these locales, which they made sites of trade and crop production.

Kaiping and Dadu, as built by Khubilai, were the largest practical examples of such citadels, in both size and organization. The former, marking the southernmost boundary of the steppes, was the summer capital—the citadel of the summer pastures. The latter, being the northernmost extent of the agricultural lands, was the winter capital. Khubilai and the Great Khans after him traveled annually between both capitals leading an imperial court and an army, as though binding together the nomadic and agricultural regions.

Some three hundred fifty kilometers separated the two capitals, placing the area partly in both the nomadic and agricultural regions. The area became the metropolitan region of the Dai-ön Uls, in which central military, political, and economic functions were concentrated. Communities equipped with production facilities and warehouses were located here, as were military bases and government-run ranches.

Nor were such building programs limited to this metropolitan region. Rulers under Khubilai on the Mongolian Plateau and Zhongyuan also built citadels in their summer and winter quarters. Many of these rulers also retained spheres of nomadic political control which included settled peoples.

The isolation of these zones halved their significance. They needed each other for connection, communication, and exchange.

The Mongol expansion enabled long-range east-west trade over the Pamirs. Normalizing such trade would require stability in the traffic of people and caravans, the transport of people and cargo, and in distribution networks. Facilities to underpin these requirements would likewise be necessary.

The *jamchi* network that spanned Eurasia, as shown in Figure 22 (p. 123), was the utmost exponent of such infrastructure. It provided the arteries from which numerous lines branched. It was the fullest expression of the Mongol polity as protector of traders.

Commerce and Tax Collection

The government of Khubilai thereby turned its attention to building the means for stably and organically forging bonds between nomads and farmers, migratory and settled populations. We can treat buildings and infrastructure as described above as hard measures, and organization and policy as soft measures. This administration introduced innovations in this latter regard as well as the former.

One prominent adviser to Khubilai was economic affairs bureaucrat Ahmad Fanakati (d. 1282). He was a Muslim merchant of Iranian descent, one of a people who, as described previously, had once formed a financial concern that had controlled the economic sphere from the Pamirs westward, and had close ties with nomadic regimes. These people had been quick to follow the Uyghur merchants of Sogdian descent, who had dominated business circles east from the Pamirs, in swearing allegiance to the Mongols. Together, these peoples maintained the financial affairs of this constantly growing regime. They also turned those financial affairs into opportunities to increase their own profits.

Persian was the Eurasian lingua franca of the time because the extensive and energetic activities of these Iranian Muslims had the greatest impact. The situation was similar to that of English today.

These merchants operated from the grassland and oasis regions. Thus, by allying themselves with the Mongols they expanded the range of transactions they handled. The capital they controlled also steadily increased in scale. At least two distinctive features can be discerned.

The first is the type of business. As the merchants' capital grew, much business came to be conducted as joint investments. These were called *ortogh* in Turkic, which can mean "group," "partner," or "association." It connoted the same idea as "partnership" or "company" in the West—in other words, a corporate enterprise. Businesses were also diversifying, becoming what some would call "general trading companies."

The Khubilai administration instituted government offices with jurisdiction over these *ortogh* concerns. It might be more accurate to say that the *ortogh* simply assumed the status of government offices, whereupon the executives of these *ortogh* doubled as bureaucrats. Having come under Mongol protection, they made use of Mongol governmental apparatus.

In return, the *ortogh* paid the Mongol government a portion of their profits in the form of taxes. In addition to defraying public works, these taxes were distributed by Khubilai imperial grants to influential people such as nobles and aristocrats. In either case, these funds would be reinvested in the *ortogh*. The administration and the businesses thus preserved economic order as a unified whole and promoted investment.

Most taxes were thereby collected from long-range commercial distribution processes, in what is known as *tamya* (*tamgha*). The word means "seal" in Mongol and Turkic, and was frequently interpreted to mean "trade tax" in Chinese at the time. A more precise interpretation would be levies in a broader sense, including taxes on monopolies as well as a general trading tax.

It became accepted practice to entirely subcontract the collection of these levies to large businesses that were close to the government. This was probably the handiest and least expensive method, both for the merchants who bore the tax burden and for the administration that made the collections. In any event, Khubilai's administration hardly ever contemplated taxing agriculture. These taxes were a conception of a nomadic regime allied with commercial capital.

Currency Systems

Another distinctive feature is the substance of the funds being thus moved around as investments and taxes. When engaging in trade with a wide variety of parties, a currency is needed which everyone will accept as payment. Silver served this purpose at the time. It was an international currency, foreign exchange, used primarily westward by the Iranian Muslim merchants.

As the power of the Mongols expanded, the use of silver as currency spread throughout the East as well. The commercial capital supplied the taxes of the government, and silver was thus necessary for levying and paying taxes as well as settling transactions. A silver-standard state economy extending over a wide area east and west was thus established under Mongol rule.

As it was still a scarce precious metal, silver was not feasible to use in all circumstances. This was especially true in the East, where there was no tradition of using silver as money.

Prior to the Yuan, coins of copper and iron, as well as paper currency, had circulated in the East (i.e., East Asia). The earliest Chinese coins had come into general use during the Tang-Song transition. Large-scale transactions became increasingly frequent as the economy became more advanced, necessitating a more practical payment medium than coins of these varieties.

Paper currency came into use as a result. Chinese political entities, whether the Jin or the Southern Song, struggled with maintaining the faith and credit of paper money, which had originated as negotiable paper instruments. The raising of specie reserve to be exchanged for paper money and the withdrawal of paper money from circulation did not always go well.

Khubilai's government overcame these problems. Silver, which was also used in trade transactions in the East, was established as a convertible currency, and paper money was likewise established as a key currency. The convertibility of paper money to gold and silver was guaranteed, and the government mandated that taxes were to be paid in paper money. These measures made it possible to adjust the amount of money in circulation, simplifying its management.

The commercial capital, which managed finances and taxation for the government, kept things running smoothly. So long as it controlled the

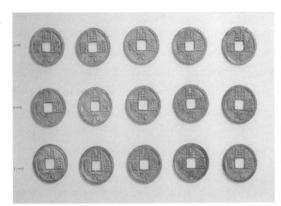

Early Chinese Currency (Chinese Copper Coin Standard)
Reproduced from Okamoto Takashi, *Chugoku keizaishi* [An Economic History of China] (Nagoya: University of Nagoya Press, 2013). Original photo in *To shi Dorakubo: Genshu rengo kokotai hakkutsu chosa hokokusho 1* [The Tomb of Shi Daoluo of the Tang Dynasty: Excavation Report of the Joint Archaeological Team of Yuanzhou] (Tokyo: Bensei Publishing, 1999), part 1.

Paper Currency of the Mongol Empire
Photo courtesy of the Currency Museum of the Bank of Japan.

Currency in the Mongol Era

issuance and withdrawal from circulation of paper money and kept the supply and demand of that paper money in balance, the commercial capital was able to preserve the currency's value. The commercial economy thus became even more energized.

This systemization of commerce, taxation, and money soon reached even Jiangnan after the defeat of the Southern Song, which held out the longest against capitulating to the Mongols. The Mongols levied trade taxes on Jiangnan, including a *tamgha* tax on the salt monopoly there. The revenues from these taxes bankrolled the increased purchasing power of the Huabei farmland and the grassland region, with Dadu situated at their core. Rice and other grains and staples from Jiangnan thus traveled northward, with paper money brought into Jiangnan as payment. Jiangnan merchants turned the paper money into funds for wholesale purchases which they allocated to producers. The paper money was then returned to the central authority by means of renewed *tamgha* tax payments. So long as this cycle remained unbroken, the public finances of the North and the industry in Jiangnan both kept expanding their operations, and the circulation of paper money became increasingly commonplace.

During and after the reign of Khubilai, the Mongol Empire, having halted its military expansion, instead broke new ground in economics and raised the world to a new stage. Long-range commerce, the silver standard economy, taxation on distribution, and contracting the collection of such taxes would be essential in defining the structure and advancement of Asian history to come.

3. The Post-Mongol Period

From Land to Sea

The Mongol regime began life as a preeminent military force. Having unified the majority of Eurasia militarily and politically in the early half of the thirteenth century, the Mongols allied with the commercial capital during the process of that unification. In the latter half of the century they built new systems, and in a sense reinvented themselves as an economic state. The state's spheres of exchange and economy were much larger than the scope of its complete political control. Those other spheres encompassed practically the whole of the Eurasian region of the time.

Though the Mongol Empire began as a strictly military regime, it underwent a significant conversion in Khubilai's period. The view of Eurasia was one in which the entire region—despite the remaining political plurality of and latent conflict between individual areas—had become a single economic exchange zone united by commerce. The monetary system and distributive organization that Khubilai's administration devised in partnership with the Silk Road commercial capital contributed to this development in no small degree.

This zone eventually extended to a maritime as well as a land-based domain. As the might of the Mongols reached the coasts, the land-based commercial capital and economic sphere that kept close company with the state established trade links with Muslim merchants who had long been operating primarily in the Indian Ocean. As a political entity, the Mongols attempted to organize these ties in what could be described as the application and extension of their alliance with the commercial capital.

The Muslim merchants' existing maritime trade network extended individually to the East China Sea. A Muslim community had already been established in ports on the Jiangnan coast, for instance. An exemplar of these merchants was Pu Shougeng, who resided in Quanzhou from the Southern Song to the Dai-ön Uls and exercised great influence.

Siding with the Dai-ön Uls, Pu Shougeng participated in the fall of the Southern Song and devoted himself to prosperity in trade. The historical record embodies how he linked the Mongol Empire with Muslim maritime commerce. Kuwabara Jitsuzo (1871–1931), a pioneer in the field of Eastern historical studies, elucidated the full scope of commerce on the seas around China through his research, as documented in the book *Ho Juko no jiseki* (The Exploits of Pu Shougeng). He is further renowned for having elevated the discipline of Eastern historical studies in Japan to world-class status.

Some hypotheses suggest that the Mongol invasions of 1274 and 1281, in which the Mongols attempted to conquer Japan by sea, were part of this overall effort to find new maritime markets. It is true that while Japan and the Mongols were hostile to one another politically, nongovernmental commerce and exchange became active between them thereafter. The Japanese archipelago thereby at last became an actor on the stage of world history. The Mongol invasions of Japan of 1274 and 1281 and their repulse symbolized this development.

This happened during the time of the Mongol deployment into the China Seas. The Mongols and their associated forces had also long been making inroads into the Mediterranean, which was a far more active and prosperous route. They were accordingly involved in the Crusades, and began shaping economic relations so as to encompass the West.

"The Crisis of the Fourteenth Century"

Political and military archives are readily preserved, making them conspicuous in historical terms. Many of these records are of short-term affairs, however. The greater the impact on—or the significance to—later times, the harder it is to retrospectively judge that impact or significance. On the other hand, while there are fewer direct accounts of economic or cultural matters, their impact is much clearer when seen from a distance as a situation developing over a long period of time. The economic unification of Eurasia, as described here, removed any doubt about the strong influence the Mongols would have on times to come.

At the time, however, clouds soon gathered. This was early in the latter half of the fourteenth century.

The climate, which had been warming since the tenth century, began cooling again. Natural disasters and diseases occurred and spread globally. The plagues that struck Europe are the best-known instances. What would later be called the "Crisis of the Fourteenth Century" had arrived.

Disasters and epidemics pose a great threat even in modern times. People often have little choice but to resign themselves to the harm caused by such events. It was effectively impossible to overcome such a crisis using the systems and organizations of the fourteenth century.

The situation in the Mongol period was even worse. The Mongol unification of Eurasia was the result of a continual expansion of factors suited to the times, including technological innovation, increased productivity, and growth in transportation, commerce, and distribution. All of these had capitalized on the then-current period of global warming.

All of the Eurasian Mongol regimes collapsed during the Crisis of the Fourteenth Century. In China, rebellions occurred that marked the end of the Yuan dynasty and the rise of the Ming dynasty. The Dai-ön Uls lost Jiangnan and Zhongyuan in succession, withdrew from Dadu, and retreated to the Mongolian Plateau.

Consequently, the systems that were supposed to unify the grassland and agricultural regions were shattered. The region's economy hit rock bottom as well.

It is no exaggeration to say that Eurasian unification was lost forever. At the very least, no record was left to history of anything similar happening from the Mongol collapse to the present. There have been vectors of growth in power and unification from inland to the coasts like those the Mongol Empire achieved. But since the fall of the Mongols, noteworthy movements have if anything moved mainly in the opposite direction.

Prior Asian historical regional structures set the outlines of the ranges that each *uls* of the Mongol Empire governed. Whereas the Mongols had unified the whole of Eurasia, the government of each *uls* at the territory level formed the foundation for future organization by their groups. The Asian ecological regional structure shown in Figure 4 (p. 39) was thus actualized into sociopolitical regions.

Due to the Crisis of the Fourteenth Century, these regions lost the bonds that joined them together. They accordingly became increasingly independent from each other. A clear tendency toward division and breakup emerged, solidifying the configuration of subsequent Asian history. There has been a trend among some historians to call this era the "post-Mongol period."

Chaghatai Turkic and the Timurid Dynasty

We begin our survey with the heart of the Mongol Empire: Central Asia, the core zone of the Silk Road. Under Mongol rule, this region corresponded to the Chaghatai Uls.

Here, the Mongols, on their westward advance, blended into and became one with the large Turkic Muslim population. Persian had been the common language in the area since the time of the Sogdians of Iranian descent, who had lived there since before Turkification and Islamization. As Iranian merchants had been an international conglomerate with consistent control of commerce and finance, their language, Persian, became the lingua franca of the Mongol period as well. This was especially true in Central Asia and points west.

After the Turkification of Central Asia, a written language was established centered on the newly arrived Turkic language, with vocabulary and grammar added from Persian and Arabic. This language was known as Chaghatai Turkic.

Central Asia occupies a strategic point—at the crossroads of East and West—and is prone to separate into eastern and western parts. The establishment of Islam under Mongol rule at last resulted in a single culture taking root there. After the collapse of the Chaghatai Uls, the Hülegü Uls, and the rest of the Mongol polities, Timur (also known in the West as Tamerlane) (1336–1405) emerged. From his capital at Samarkand, he extended his power in all directions, and built a great empire.

This empire, the Timurid dynasty, was the undoubted successor of the Western half of the Mongol Empire. The structure of the entity hewed closely to that of the Mongols as well. This dynasty at the functional center of the world enjoyed prosperity in the fifteenth century. With Chaghatai Turkic literature forming its core, a great civilization blossomed and gloried in Herat, Samarkand, and other key oasis cities.

That prosperity and civilization did not last long, and when the Timurid dynasty fell, the region fragmented into Uzbek regimes which rose and fell independently of one another. This unstable political situation persisted, and its foundations steadily weakened.

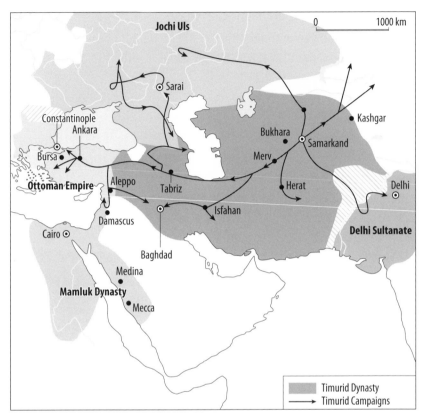

Fig. 23. The Timurid Dynasty in the 15th Century

Economic conditions were likely associated with this state of affairs. The caravan trade which supported the region presumably forged ties with each of the various regimes, and profited and flourished as best it could. But it was unable to restore the importance and pervasiveness that it had had up until the Mongol period. Thereafter, maritime trade expanded, leading to the Age of Discovery. Overland caravan trade could only decline by comparison.

The trails and travels of Babur (1483–1530), inheritor of the Timurid bloodline, tell the story. Defeated in political strife in Central Asia, Babur traveled southward through Afghanistan, seeking a new world in Hindustan. There he founded the Mughal dynasty, and the economic prosperity of India, which depended on the seas, assured that dynasty's rise and success.

In the course of Indian history, there had been more than a few nomadic regimes that had moved southward from Central Asia to rule Northern India. The Mughals were the latest iteration of those waves of nomads. The nomadic forces of the people of Chaghatai may have extended their power as far as India. This particular instance, however, was intimately connected to the comparative foundational collapse in neighboring Central Asia. There would be no more southern reigns of nomadic forces after the founding of the Mughal dynasty.

That this historical process of nomads founding southern dominions would not be repeated was likely a situation unprecedented in history, and signaled the start of a new historical period. We might reasonably think of this new period as the origin of the Great Game between England and Russia, which began in the latter half of the nineteenth century and played out in India and Central Asia, as well as the conquest and partition of Central Asia and Turkistan thereafter by the Russians and the Han Chinese.

The Formation of Iran

After the fall of the Timurid dynasty, the Iran *zamin*, the lands south and west of the Amu River that were primarily inhabited by Iranians, moved closer to merging into a single state. Broadly speaking, the scope of this region had corresponded to the now-defunct Hülegü Uls, which had been succeeded by the Safavid dynasty.

This dynasty was founded in the time of Ismail I (1487–1524), in the early half of the sixteenth century. At Merv in Khorasan, Ismail destroyed the Shaybanid dynasty, which had overthrown the Timurid dynasty. Having arrested the southern advance of Shaybanid forces, Ismail brought stability to Safavid rule.

Following the Islamization and Turkification of Central Asia around the eleventh century, Turkic and Mongol nomadic armies repeatedly advanced south and west into West Asia. The growth of the Seljuk and

Khwarezm-Shah dynasties was a manifestation of these waves, as were Hülegü's western campaigns and Timur's conquests.

Taking the long view, the victory of the Safavid dynasty was a historical turnabout: a watershed event in which these uninterrupted waves from Central Asia were stopped at last. With the concurrent emergence and rise of the Ottoman Empire immediately to the west of the Safavid dynasty, the western part of Eurasia started to become more stable.

The Safavid dynasty reinstituted the title of Shah for its rulers, in its quest to restore ancient Persia. Additionally, the dynasty adopted the Twelver Shi'ah sect of Islam as its official faith. Briefly stated, this is the largest Shia group today, and it holds that Muslim leadership is established through twelve imams starting with Muhammad's cousin Ali, rather than the caliphs. Shiism remains firmly rooted to this day in Iran and Azerbaijan, which are politically and culturally distinct from the rest of the Islamic world. This trend would prove a decisive turning point in the course of the Safavid dynasty, though we should not exaggerate its importance before its proper time.

The Safavids, the Mughals, Central Asia, and the Ottomans (about whom more later) were all adjacent. Hence, more often than not, they fell into political and military conflict with one another. However, the peoples thrived with the commonalities of Islam and Persian culture among

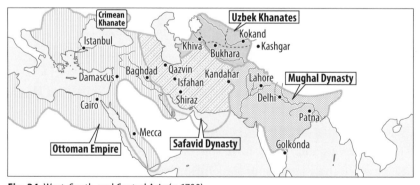

Fig. 24. West, South, and Central Asia (c. 1700)
Adapted from Morimoto Kazuo, ed., *Perushia-go ga musunda sekai: Mo hitotsu no Yurashia shi* [The World Connected by the Persian Language: Another Eurasian History] (Sapporo: Hokkaido University Press, 2009), 10.

themselves as a medium of movement and intercourse, as depicted in Figure 24. A balanced, stable order was maintained there through the latter half of the eighteenth century.

The Safavid dynasty was built on the nomadic army of the Azerbaijan Steppe. As Azerbaijan had previously been the home base of the Hülegü Uls, the Safavid dynasty patterned its organizational structure closely on that of this predecessor.

That is to say, the Safavids made Turkic and Mongol nomadic military force the core of their authority. Influential Turkic and Mongol tribes held the real power in the lands of the dynasty's domain. At the same time, Iranian settlers in the area attended to civil government, managed economic functions, and supported the ruling state. The dynasty shared this power structure with the Timurid dynasty before it and, in a larger sense, with the Mongol Empire, including East Asia.

After the breakup of the Timurid dynasty, which had been the Western successor to the Mongol Empire, we could say that the center of gravity had shifted to the southern coasts, becoming the domain of the Mughal dynasty in India and the Safavid dynasty in Iran. This change would signify the beginning of another historical period.

The Ottoman Empire

The Arabic world that lay to Iran's west—Syria and points West from there—was the sphere of the Sunni, the Muslim majority. But it was not uniform otherwise. The Turkic nomadic forces that had repeatedly invaded from eastward were holding their ground. There were also more than a few Christians who had been there since Roman times, in both European and Asian regions, and some remaining Mongol forces. The Ottoman Empire suddenly arose in the midst of all of these.

The Ottoman Empire originated as a band of Turkic nomads in Anatolia. Gradually increasing in power, they advanced into the Balkans in the mid-fourteenth century and made Christian states capitulate to them in succession. Thus, the Ottomans, having become the preeminent power in Anatolia, conquered Constantinople in 1453, growing even larger. Following this conquest, Mehmed II moved the Ottoman capital to Constantinople, which he officially renamed Istanbul. The name Constantinople remained in common use, however, and is used in this book as well.

Constantinople is a geopolitically strategic point, where Asia, Europe, the Black Sea, and the Mediterranean meet. It is well known to history that the Crusades strove mightily to seize Constantinople in order to control the Mediterranean. Accordingly, the conquest of the city attests to the Ottoman Empire's having grown into a great power that commanded the Eastern Mediterranean.

Not only that, Constantinople was also the capital of the Eastern Roman—or Byzantine—Empire. That the Ottoman Empire relocated its seat of power to Constantinople was tantamount to the empire's becoming the master of what had been the capital of the Roman Empire since the fourth century, and attaining legitimacy as the successor to both Alexander the Great and the Roman emperors who followed him.

Moreover, the Ecumenical Patriarchate of Constantinople, the highest authority in the Eastern Orthodox Church, had long been located in the imperial capital. Regardless of the self-consciousness of Ottoman emperors or government, in this way the Ottoman Empire took on the added legitimacy of mastery over both Christians and Jews.

In the early sixteenth century, the Ottoman Empire brought Mecca and Medina, the two holy places of Islam, under its management. The Ottomans thereby fulfilled the function of protecting those who made the pilgrimage required of all Muslims to these cities. The Ottoman Empire also thus gained the position and authority of being the center of Islam, and came to reign over Muslims.

Furthermore, in order to confront the various Mongol regimes to its east, the Ottoman Empire needed to secure legitimacy of a Mongol sort as well. The Ottoman takeover of the Crimean khanate, which traced its lineage back to Genghis, was a textbook case. The Ottoman imperial household frequently professed its blood relations with the lineage of Genghis. At the same time, it revered the pedigree of the Crimean khanate, even going so far as to appoint the royal family of the khanate as its successor should the Ottoman imperial line die out.

The Ottoman Empire continued to expand, becoming a mighty power that spanned Asia, Africa, and Europe, because it had singlehandedly acceded to the Roman, Islamic, and Mongol legacies. That was how a Turkic regime, which was decidedly not a majority faction, was able to reign and promulgate government over diverse peoples across a vast area.

Developments in Early Modern Asia

Such circumstances were not unique to the Ottoman Empire. Though particulars of conditions and degree varied, there were many features in common with the likes of the Mughal and Safavid dynasties. The Mughals, being descended from the lineage of Chaghatai, reigned over majority-Hindu India, while the Safavid dynasty, itself another Turkic polity, governed Iranian society.

It was no coincidence that these entities had aspects in common. They were all Islamic, and they likewise had many similarities in their social and political structures. Chiefly, all of these entities had communities consisting of rulers of nomadic origin that managed political and military matters on the one hand, and of settled peoples that were in charge of economic and cultural affairs on the other. Elites versed in both situations connected the rulers and the settled peoples, forming government overall. As this format was established by the Mongol Empire, these entities are referred to as "post-Mongol."

These polities maintained a degree of coherence in their scope of governance, from their political systems above to their ways of life below. This was despite their diversity of language, religion, and customs. It was "live and let live," whether among religious sects, between clergy and laity, or between politics and religion.

Islam was accommodating in this regard. In these times, heartbreaking incidents carried out repeatedly by Muslim fundamentalists and extremists draw our attention, leading many to see Islam as an exclusionary, intolerant religion. To be sure, present-day interpretations of doctrine and patterns of behavior warrant consideration as clear and present risks. In historical terms, however, Islamic polities were predicated on being inclusive of other religions from a legal standpoint.

Therefore, rulers could adequately rule over Christians or Hindus simply by bringing subjects of different religions to heel. In addition to Islam's inclusiveness, as mentioned previously, both the Safavid dynasty and the Ottoman Empire adopted strategies that enhanced their legitimacy by combining it with universality. Both entities thereby contrived to make their respective governance more harmonious than it would otherwise have been. The Safavid dynasty restored the ancient Persian title of shah for its rulers, and the Ottoman Empire relocated its capital to Constantinople, styling itself the successor to the Roman Empire and the guardian of the Eastern Orthodox Church.

From our viewpoint—the viewpoint of modern peoples accustomed to Western modes of thought—this state of affairs would seem an undifferentiated mixing of ethnicities or a mingling of religions. Such thinking, however, is nothing more than contempt born of values inseparable from modernistic preconceptions of "ethnicity" and "religion."

In West, Central, and South Asia, grassland nomads and settled farmers mixed together. Such mixing was the rational thing in the prevailing environmental and social conditions, in order to promote peaceful coexistence and harmonious governance to the extent practicable. We might say that many legitimacies and universalities were combined and stratified.

Even when unification was achieved in the interiors of West, Central, and South Asia, however, everything no longer cohered into a single entity, which it once had with the Mongol Empire or Timurid dynasty, as previously described. The relative economic and cultural importance of the Silk Road, which had connected these disparate groups, had declined, overcome by a centrifugal force.

That centrifugal force was on the coasts and pulled from outside these various regions. While I have given the rise of the Mughals in India as a classic example, there is another case study that would be even more comprehensible to Japanese. I refer of course to East Asia, Japan's nearest neighbor.

4. The Ming-Qing Transition and the Age of Discovery

The Founding of the Ming Dynasty

After the fall of the Mongol Empire, its remnants in the post-Mongol west survived for the most part. In Central Asia, India, and West Asia, structures were built in which migrating nomads and settled farmers were amalgamated, the Mongol structure and Islam were syncretized, and systems of pluralistic coexistence were reorganized and preserved.

While there were variations in the constituent elements, and in the combinations—the Turkic peoples with Iran, and the Arab world with the Roman world—the underlying principles binding them were the same. They were systems under which the religious universalisms and political legitimacies of different regions could coexist harmoniously. This was true of the Timurid dynasty in the fifteenth century, as well as later polities: the Ottoman Empire (during and after the fifteenth century), the Mughal dynasty, and the Safavid dynasty.

East Asia, however, was slightly different. This area was ruled by the Dai-ön Uls, where the Great Khans descended from Khubilai Khan once reigned. It was also the heart and center of the economic system that spread over the whole of Eurasia, embracing Jiangnan, which at the time was the most affluent part of the world.

The Crisis of the Fourteenth Century profoundly scarred East Asia. The Dai-ön Uls fell apart. It was no different in this regard from the regions to its west. The various regions to the south and west of the Pamirs were rapidly reunified starting with the Timurid dynasty. By contrast, East Asia as a whole remained divided for a prolonged period.

The overriding reason was the birth of the Ming dynasty, with its anti-Mongol national policy and traditions. Founded in 1368, this entity confronted the Mongols across the Great Wall for some three hundred years.

Being anti-Mongol did not mean simply taking political positions that were irreconcilable with the Mongol Empire and being in a confrontational relationship with it. The Ming dynasty adopted structures that ran counter to the very system of pluralistic coexistence between the grassland nomads and the settled farming peoples that the Mongol Empire and the Dai-ön Uls had devised. In effect, the Ming rejected the long-range commercial distribution that formed the basis of the Mongol coexistence. Instead, the Ming enacted policies that included extreme regulation of trade and an in-kind economy that was anti-commerce and anti-money. In this economic structure, goods were prioritized over currency in transactions.

This policy line on the part of the Ming was grounded at least somewhat in the reality of the state of crisis of the time, with civil disorder and stagnating crop production owing to natural disasters and warfare, as well as atrophying commerce and distribution and the breakdown of the currency system. The Ming perception was that rebuilding order amid such extreme depression and chaos required strengthened regulation of the social economy. In less abstract terms, the aim of the Ming was to recover civil order by limiting traffic and to stimulate an agricultural revival through restraint of commerce. Thus, they arrived at a system with the opposite vector of the Dai-ön Uls.

Homogenizing "Chinese-ness"

Such was the process of creating a new polity, one heavily shaped by certain inescapable aspects of its character. The Ming dynasty was founded in Jiangnan, heart of the former Southern Song dynasty that had resisted Khubilai to the last. The Ming established itself by expelling the Mongols from Dadu. It was therefore most expedient for the Ming to assert its raison d'être by way of rejecting the Mongols and the Dai-ön Uls.

The Ming accordingly utilized the Confucianist conception, which originated with the Han, of revering that which was "Chinese" and disparaging others as "barbarians." The uniqueness of the Ming lay in their persistent incorporation of this conception into their actual policies and systems, not stopping merely at the level of slogan or ideology.

The Mongol period included numerous phases in which, under the aegis of the Dai-ön Uls, various ethnic groups coexisted and amalgamated pluralistically in East Asia and mainland China, as with Central and West Asia. However, there was no assurance that ecological structures would be the same. East Asia can be more sharply divided than West Asia into either north and south or northwest and southeast parts.

The south or southeast part is the zone of settled farmers with a humid monsoon climate. The north or northwest part is the zone of nomadic herders with an arid climate. Only in Zhongyuan—that is, on the Huabei Plateau of the Huang He Basin—where farming is carried out despite the arid climate, have the respective powers of north and south met, mixed, and wrangled. The region has repeatedly made great shifts in the course of East Asian history as a result.

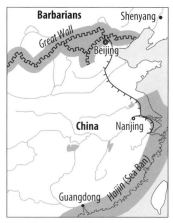

Fig. 25. The Ming Domain
Based on Okamoto Takashi, *Chugoku "han-Nichi" no genryu* [Origins of "Anti-Japaneseness" in China] (Tokyo: Kodansha, 2011), 41.

The Ming dynasty began in Jiangnan, and from there annexed Zhongyuan. They attempted to integrate the humid farming region of Jiangnan with the arid region of Zhongyuan, with its mix of nomads and farmers, and thereby to establish a homogeneous "Han China" state. To that end, they embarked on building the Great Wall, to separate and isolate the "Chinese" farmers from the "barbarian" nomads.

In addition to such land-based restrictions, the Ming also enacted strict regulations on maritime trade and traffic, making the coast a prohibited area. This was their so-called Haijin, or Sea Ban, meaning that "not a single scrap of wood may be allowed to float on the sea." This was another way in which the Ming were determined to establish a homogeneous "China."

Thus, in the post-Mongol East, in accordance with their ecologies, the classical Chinese/Confucianist sphere of southeast "China" and the northwest Mongol sphere found themselves opposing one another across the Great Wall. Tibetan Buddhism had begun to proliferate in the Mongol sphere, reinforcing the trend of north-south separatism in terms of religion and tradition as well as ecology. In the comparatively brief period of some two hundred years between the end of the fourteenth century and the end of the sixteenth century, both spheres coexisted in confrontation while increasing the homogeneity of their respective sides.

Commercialization of Society

Such coexistence was not always peaceful. Given that the Ming styled themselves as "Chinese," everyone around them had to be lower-class "barbarians." The resulting Ming attempts to make the Mongols and other states render vassal servitude, by force of arms when necessary, meant that fires of civil disorder were perpetually smoldering on the Ming periphery.

Economic trends gave impetus to such unrest. Soon after their enactment, the anti-commerce, anti-money in-kind taxation and extreme regulation of trade that the Ming had originated failed. Such policies could never have been the norm, no matter how dire the economic depression or how much commerce had declined in the crisis of the latter half of the fourteenth century.

The Chinese money economy and distribution of commodities had taken root to one degree or another prior to the tenth century, beginning with the Tang-Song transition. The in-kind taxation and regulation of trade were anachronisms, nothing more. And the situation only escalated.

Beginning in the fifteenth century, in the Jiangnan Delta, centering on Suzhou, silk and cotton handicrafts came into prominence, agricultural products were increasingly commodified, and development of previously undeveloped lands progressed, advancing specialization and interdependence among regions. Movement of people and goods was revitalized, and Chinese society as a whole became more commercial and fluid.

The money that should have been present with such active distribution was absent, however, due to the in-kind system that was in place. A lack of gold and silver ore meant that even substituting precious metals for currency necessitated obtaining them from overseas.

The demand for trade suddenly intensified. Gold and silver were needed to drive the economy, and acquiring these metals required trade.

However, the Ming prohibited the use of gold and silver as well as private-sector trade. These were against the law. The private sector engaged in trade using silver regardless. The manufacture of such attractive specialty goods as silk, cotton, tea, and ceramics caught on, eventually overflowing from domestic markets and stoking longings in foreign lands. At the same time, China had an insatiable demand for money. Practically speaking, people inside and outside China alike disregarded the Ming structure and policies—specifically, the integration and homogenization of "Chinese-ness."

"Mongols to the North, Japanese to the South"

The economic interests of Chinese and others thus aligned, and they began building combined "Chinese" and "barbarian" colonies along the coast and the Great Wall, places which the Ming had declared off-limits to segregate these groups. Even so, the Ming clung to its existing system and refused to authorize trade. When the Ming implemented and intensified enforcement against and suppression of trade by treating it as smuggling, traders had no choice but to resist, even if it meant resorting to weapons. Conflict thus continued more or less unabated, and civil order deteriorated still further, on the Ming periphery.

On the coast such activity was collectively referred to as *wako* (C. *wokou*). While literally meaning "Japanese pirates," such pirates of course needed the collusion and collaboration of the Chinese in order to conduct business. In the mid-sixteenth century, incidents of armed conflict occurred between the Ming authorities and a smuggling ring comprising both Chinese and foreigners. These were the Jiajing *wokou* raids.

The situation was not confined to the southeast. To the north, smuggling was flourishing over the Great Wall that isolated the nomadic region. The trade there was primarily in nomads' horses and Chinese teas. As along the southeastern coast, in this area disturbances persisted, opposition escalated, and there was even a mighty invasion by the Mongol host that involved a siege of Beijing. And as people south of the Great Wall also participated, the invasion could not be considered purely nomadic.

This incident too occurred in the mid-sixteenth century, at nearly the same time as the Jiajing *wokou* raids. Accordingly, the Ming designated these foreign troubles as *"beilu nanwo,"* or "Mongols to the north, Japanese to the south": threats from Mongol nomads to the north and from Japanese *wokou* pirates to the south.

The real threat, however, was the situation wrought by the Ming's attitude of clinging to the system on which their dynasty was founded. By this time, the dynasty had become an economy and society that required interaction with the outside world. Nonetheless, the Ming stubbornly persisted in "Chinese" homogenization and self-segregation from "barbarians." Their adherence to their old ways, which were on the verge of collapse, resulted in the Ming bringing these threats down on themselves.

On the other hand, both the "Mongols to the north" and the "Japanese to the south" were multiethnic pluralistic groups or societies, without regard for notions of interior or exterior, "Chinese" or "barbarian." A new force, a new political entity, emerged in these groups, one that would inaugurate a new era. This was the Qing dynasty, an assemblage chiefly of Manchus with Mongols and Han. With the advent of the Qing, East Asia would at last steer a course toward coexistence and unification after more than two hundred years of continual schism, confrontation, and disorder.

The Rise and Achievements of the Qing

The Manchus were originally an armed trading concern in the Liaodong region. They lived between the Han people of the Ming dynasty and the Mongols of the grasslands. In the early seventeenth century they rose to power, reigning over the Mongols, succeeding the Ming, which had fallen due to internal conflict, and organizing East Asia into a single political entity. Calling themselves Daicing Gurun (Great Qing), the Manchus patterned themselves as the inheritors of Khubilai's Dai-ön

Uls. In this way, they became the next post-Mongol empire, following the Ottoman Empire and the Mughal dynasty.

Such governments used to be called "conquest dynasties." And the term certainly fits here, in the sense that these were all remnants of the Mongols that combined various kinds of legitimacy and universality while enforcing minority rule.

Of course, the internal organization of the Qing dynasty was not entirely the same as that of the Mongol Empire, nor that of the later western regimes. Islam, with its tolerance of other religions, had gained little foothold in East Asia, while the classical Chinese language sphere, which in union with Confucianism sharply distinguishes boundaries between self and other and discriminates between in-group and out-group, was well established. This made pluralistic coexistence much more difficult than it was in the later Western regimes. There was also the great

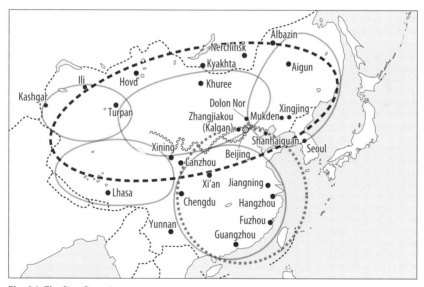

Fig. 26. The Qing Domain
The bold dashed oval is the arid interior zone with the Mongol and Tibetan Buddhist spheres at its core. The gray dashed circle encompasses both the Confucianist-classical Chinese sphere and the humid coastal monsoon zone. The five gray circles, clockwise from top left, indicate territories inhabited by Muslims, Mongols, Manchus, Han Chinese, and Tibetans.

north-south disparity: ecological conditions were completely different between the humid coastal monsoon zones and the arid interior zones. Hence, beliefs and customs also differed between them.

For this reason, the Qing sovereigns ruled simultaneously as Great Khans of the Mongols, who were devotees of Tibetan Buddhism, and as emperors of China. In the northwest, they conducted themselves as sovereigns of the Mongols and grand patrons of Tibetan Buddhism, whereas they presented themselves to the Han of the southeast as being defenders of Confucianism, as well as being the greatest Chinese intellectuals.

This method of governing by combining legitimacy and universality was the same as that practiced in India and West Asia. The north-south separation in beliefs and customs, which derived from their respective ecological conditions, was far too great in East Asia, however, necessitating this composite of different forms of government with hardly any connection whatsoever. There would be little later interaction among Han Chinese, Mongols, and Tibetans, with mutual awareness among them becoming increasingly distanced. Nonetheless, at the time, this was the optimal means for peaceful management of East Asia. One might say that the achievement of the Qing was to serve out its time consistently as one personage in these dual overlapping roles of different rulers and regimes.

Maritime Trade

In this way, the Qing was born from the melting pot of internal and external mixing known as "Mongols to the north, Japanese to the south." The Qing was thus able to unify anew a pluralistic East Asia as had been previously achieved by the Dai-ön Uls.

This "Mongols to the north, Japanese to the south" situation took definite shape in the sixteenth century, when the world entered the Age of Discovery. These circumstances were clearly connected.

Vasco da Gama (c. 1469–1524) and Christopher Columbus (c. 1451–1506) "discovered" the sea routes to India and the Americas in the late fifteenth century. Thereafter, world history, which had played out almost exclusively on the Eurasian continent, shifted to a global story encompassing the whole of the Earth. The impetus for this shift was discovery. For without voyages of discovery crossing the Indian, Pacific, and Atlantic Oceans, global history would never have begun.

Seaborne traffic and maritime trade existed prior to this time, of course. As we have previously seen, the Mediterranean had been a prime stage for world history since ancient times. It had been an inland sea for Syria, Greece, Rome, and Islam under the Umayyads, and had emerged as a trade and traffic backbone for these states. With the start of the Abbasid dynasty, the direction of Islam's force shifted eastward, and maritime trade expanded from the Mediterranean in the West to the eastern oceans. Muslim trade activities over the Indian Ocean thus flourished.

Even so, in overall terms, seaborne trade by the Muslims was still secondary. The main route for traffic and commerce on a global scale was still the Silk Road—that is, overland. The relative importance of sea routes was still not very high. The history of Eurasia was a terrestrial world history until the Mongol period. The only corresponding coast was that of the Indian Ocean; the Atlantic Ocean and the East China Sea were the ends of the Earth.

Nevertheless, seaborne trade made definite progress, and Muslim merchants had been habitually coming and going even as far as the China Seas since the Tang period. Muslim communities were also formed in various coastal areas. The significant roles that these people came to play in the Dai-ön Uls have been described in earlier chapters.

Khubilai's Dai-ön Uls made repeated attempts at seaborne campaigns, including the Mongol invasions of Japan in 1274 and 1281. Aside from military objectives, these enterprises may have been intended to unify and systematize the Muslim trade, which had been scattered from the Indian Ocean to the China Seas. If so, then we should consider the substance of the Zheng He campaigns conducted by the Ming Yongle emperor (1360–1424) in the early fifteenth century to be the same as Khubilai's seaborne expeditions, regardless of their immediate motives and objectives, given that Zheng He (c. 1371–1434) was a Muslim eunuch in the Ming court.

The Rise of India

These were the prerequisites for the sixteenth-century Age of Discovery to come about. The "discoveries" of the sea routes to India and of the Americas were based on the actions of Westerners seeking the products of "India," that is, the East. And it was the seaborne trade activities of the Muslim merchants that provided these products to the West. To paraphrase geographer Iizuka Koji (1906–1970), the "discovery" of the water route to India was merely the Portuguese "being guided by [Muslim] pilots" on a course that the Muslim merchants had long been utilizing (Iizuka, *Toyo shi to Seiyo shi to no aida*).

Thus, even the so-called Age of Discovery was, to begin with, nothing more than Europeans joining in seagoing traffic that Muslims had conducted up to that time. What mattered, however, was what came after: the emergence of the Indian Ocean and the Indian subcontinent.

Up to then, India had been disconnected from the main course of the Silk Road, even though its interactions with Central Asia were uninterrupted. In terms of Eurasia as a whole, we might say that India was even more isolated than Jiangnan, China, at the easternmost end of the continent. After the decline of the Timurid dynasty, however, the foundation of the Silk Road collapsed, relatively speaking. The grassland regions would never regain the relative importance in world history that they had commanded in bygone times.

The caravan trade that bolstered the region had not ceased to be, of course. In terms of absolute overall volume, it probably did not decline very much, and it was likely profitable as well. Compared, however, to the worldwide significance that the Silk Road had had in prior eras, or to maritime trade during and after the Age of Discovery, the Silk Road could not help but decline. Such was the rapid rise in relative importance of the seas.

Thus, the Indian Ocean went from being Eurasia's incidental coastal waters to being a principal artery of the world. Accordingly, India replaced Central Asia as the heart of Asia, the presence which swayed the course of the world, especially economically. We might say that this was a revolutionary development in world history unlike any other to that point.

Thereafter, India would become known for its appealing international products, such as cotton goods and dyes. The prosperity of seaborne trade also contributed to the economic advancement that these products successively gave rise to.

The Formation of a Global World History

The "discovery" of the sea route to India was the most important catalyst for this transition from land to sea—that is, the decline of the grasslands and the rise of the oceans. The historical record leaves no room for doubt on this point.

Even so, the preexisting seaborne trade routes would have had connections and expansions westward to the Mediterranean via the Persian Gulf and the Red Sea, and eastward to the China Seas via Southeast Asia. The "discovery" at issue was nothing more than the addition of a direct route from western Europe to India around the Cape of Good Hope. The reason this "discovery" rapidly increased in apparent importance was that it was in fact linked to another "discovery."

This was the "discovery" of the New World, though there is little meaning in the mere act of "discovery" itself. The great significance of this "discovery" lay in the presence of rich veins of silver ore and the production of vast amounts of silver there, which would be showered on the Indian Ocean, with western Europe as an interconnecting node (see Fig. 27, p. 152).

The mining development that Europeans undertook on the far side of the planet was actually for the Asian seaborne trade, and India was the first destination of the resulting silver. The trade did not stop there, however. Silver rapidly streamed into China as well, which was experiencing a society-wide increase in commercialization and fluidity. Silver circled the globe and flooded China from the East and the West alike. There are estimates that one-third of all the world's silver exports in the early seventeenth century flowed into China.

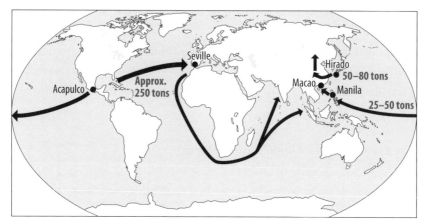

Fig. 27. The Movement of Silver (c. 1600)

In China's case, the New World and Europe were not the only sources of silver. There was a much closer source of silver in abundance: the Japanese archipelago.

The gold and silver rush of the Sengoku period (late fifteenth to sixteenth centuries) in Japan was spurred by Chinese demand for precious metals and Sino-Japanese trade. The Iwami Ginzan Silver Mine, Japan's largest, in the city of Oda in Shimane Prefecture, was designated a UNESCO World Heritage site in 2007. China and the Age of Discovery were essential conditions for Japan to rapidly become rich and powerful in the sixteenth century. On reflection, these would have furnished the historical factors that gave rise to the *wokou* of the China Seas and by extension to China's "Mongols to the north, Japanese to the south" state of affairs, as well as ultimately having brought about the advent of the Qing dynasty.

The maritime commercial boom of the Age of Discovery was of course not limited to China and the China Seas. Rather, in this regard China and the China Seas were the most backward part of the world. The Mediterranean had had this experience long before it happened even in the Indian Ocean.

In accordance with these economic circumstances, the Ottoman Empire expanded from Anatolia to the Eastern Mediterranean and the shores of the Red Sea, the Safavid dynasty turned from Azerbaijan to the Persian Gulf, and the Mughal dynasty moved from Afghanistan to Hindustan, and farther southward from there. The direction of these and the Qing expanding from the interior to the coasts is all of a piece, clearly showing the attraction of the seas. Such sources of attraction, such driving forces, are no longer to be found in Asia.

Global history is world history that links to the present—that is, to modern times. Western Europe, a region located at the farthest end of Eurasia, which heretofore made hardly any impression at all, had taken the lead role. World history was on the verge of a dramatic change.

CHAPTER 4

THE MODERN WEST

1. The Rise and Fall of Italy and the First Signs of Modern Europe

Italy and the Mediterranean

In the vocabulary of Western historical studies, the Age of Discovery was nothing less than the start of the Atlantic revolutions. It was the beginning of the rise of Western Europe together with the Americas, marking the formation of the core of the so-called world economy. The scope of that economy would not be limited to just the Atlantic region, the Western Hemisphere. It would eventually provide an opportunity to transfer the role of managers of traffic and trade on the Indian Ocean— and in fact naval supremacy itself—from the Muslims to the Europeans, particularly the Anglo-Saxons.

With this change, the weight of world history shifted decisively from Asia to Western Europe. In this sense, the Atlantic revolutions must be considered revolutions in world history. This change did not spring suddenly upon the world with the Age of Discovery, nor did it manifest in an immediately apparent form. We must be cognizant of the long history prior to this event, as well as the processes that followed.

Viewed through the scope of so-called Western history, the Age of Discovery means that the stage of Western history shifted from the Mediterranean to the Atlantic, and the leading role changed hands from Italy to Western Europe. We must begin with the previous historical stage that was the Mediterranean and the rise of its earlier leading player, Italy.

As both the Mediterranean and Italy were the heart of the old Roman Empire, it might be more appropriate to call this a revival rather than a rise. It was probably due to this nuance that French nationalist historian Jules Michelet (1798–1874) first used the term "Renaissance," which thereafter became a generalized concept.

The notion of an Italian Renaissance was itself Eurocentric, of course. Such a historical view could only arise from identifying Rome with Europe and conceiving the latter as the rightful successor of the former.

As discussed elsewhere in this book, however, the Mediterranean world and Rome were both part of the ancient Near East, not Europe. There was no such place as Europe when the Roman Empire flourished, nor would there be during the centuries of the so-called Migration period.

The foundation of the European realm began at last in 800, when the Vatican allied with Charlemagne (742–814), King of the Franks, and "restored" the Western Roman Empire. So goes the consensus of world history.

Europe and Rome

The Frankish Kingdom lay partly in Gaul and partly in Germania, an outlying corner at the cold northwestern end of Eurasia, cut off from the Mediterranean and the ancient Near East. Its domain expanded, eventually annexing northern Italy and thereby uniting with the Roman Catholic Church. Thus was an independent Europe established, though it might be appropriate to call it an isolated Europe.

Europe at the time was largely constituted by Charlemagne's "empire." In both nature and conditions, this "empire" was utterly at odds with the Roman Empire that had once proclaimed the Mediterranean to be *mare nostrum* ("our sea"). Charlemagne's "empire" could not objectively be called a "restoration" in any sense.

For its part, the Mediterranean was almost entirely controlled by the Muslims. Under the formulation that Christianity equals Europe, "the ancient Near East begins at the Pyrenees" (Iizuka, *Toyo shi to Seiyo shi to no aida*), and nearly all of the Mediterranean was part of the ancient Near East.

This situation is exemplified by the vicissitudes of Sicily. This island, occupying a strategic point near the center of the Mediterranean, was the focus of contention between ancient Rome and Carthage. It was part of the Eastern Roman Empire beginning in the reign of Justinian, and came under Islamic control in the latter half of the ninth century. This history is sufficient to show that possession of Sicily dictated domination of the Mediterranean.

The Sicilian Muslims located their central stronghold at Palermo, a town of some three thousand inhabitants. In practically no time at all, it would grow into a city of more than 300,000, making it a primary Islamic city on a par with Cairo and Cordoba—due to the thorough use the Muslims made of its advantageous position.

In the light of these geographical conditions, Rome and the whole Italian Peninsula on the Mediterranean became the center of Europe, and thus Christianity. Simultaneously, the Peninsula was also the farthest frontier of the ancient Near East and the Islamic world. These civilizations were unmistakably far more advanced than contemporary Europe. These factors provided the prerequisites for the ascent of Italy.

Sicily as Focal Point

The Western Roman Empire was one of the regions hardest hit by the climatic cooling that began in the third century. In addition to withering crop yields and economic atrophy, it brought attacks by armed refugees, the sacking of cities, destruction of infrastructure, and the decline of civilization known to history as the Migration period. It is no exaggeration to call this period the Dark Ages.

After centuries of exhaustion and stagnation, however, the first rays of hope appeared. Following hundreds of years of labor and deforestation, European agriculture became active again and crop yields began to recover. At nearly the same time, the long global cooling trend came to an end, and the world climate began to warm. This happened around the tenth century.

The development of woodlands and uncultivated lands, and increased crop yields, permitted increases in population. The medieval period or Middle Ages, beginning in the eleventh century, saw Europe's population double. From the perspective of the Italian Peninsula, this occurred in the hinterland, on the continent.

As to what had been happening on the seaside—the gateway, as seen from the Peninsula—bumper crops overflowed from farming villages, trade and distribution started up, commerce and industry began to boom, and markets and cities regained their vitality. One could say that the prosperity of Islamized Sicily under the Arabs was a forerunner of this phenomenon.

The Italian Peninsula was the frontier of the Mediterranean and the Islamic world—especially Sicily, the point of contact with the area south

Fig. 28. The Mediterranean World (c. 1150)
Reproduced from Takayama Hiroshi, *Chusei Shichiria okoku* [The Norman Kingdom of Sicily] (Tokyo: Kodansha, 1999), 103, Fig. 4-1.

of the Peninsula. Having fallen into Muslim hands and Islamized, the island enjoyed both the agricultural technologies and the urban civilization of the ancient Near East. Sicily thus built agricultural and commercial prosperity before anywhere else in Europe.

The Normans, who came from the far north, conquered both Sicily and southern Italy in the eleventh century to build the Norman kingdom of Sicily in 1130, as part of the Norman Conquest.

The maritime movements arising in this time of global warming catalyzed the expansion and comeback of Europe, which had heretofore been pushed back and isolated to Charlemagne's "empire." Control of the Mediterranean had passed from the Muslim world to Europe, owing to the Norman conquest of Syria and the Crusades. The total volume of trade in Italy thus increased dramatically, and port cities such as Pisa, Genoa, and Venice began to thrive as well.

The prosperity of Palermo continued even after it became part of the Norman kingdom of Sicily. The reason was that, even though the barbaric Normans had converted to Christianity, Palermo's governance continued unbroken from the preceding Muslim period. As the Normans were an uncomplicated people without prejudice against Muslims, they proactively employed those very Muslims and embraced their political and economic systems. This was how the Norman kingdom of Sicily managed to become the most advanced country in the Christian world.

The sun clearly began to set on Sicily near the end of the twelfth century, however. The northern Italian cities became superior in shipping and trade. The life and times of Holy Roman Emperor Frederick II (1194–1250) graphically embody this change of aspect.

Frederick II

Frederick II was the last emperor of the Hohenstaufen dynasty of the Holy Roman Empire, and is thus known by his German name. In modern categories and sentiments, however, he was an Italian through and through, and could hardly be said to have been German. He reportedly said that he wished never to live anywhere but Italy, nor speak anything but Italian.

Born to the Sicilian royal house, Frederick started out as king of Sicily, making Palermo his base. Even after being crowned Holy Roman Emperor, he paid no heed to Germany, and continued his conflict with the Roman Catholic Church. Dreaming of unifying the Italian Peninsula from the south, he fought in various domains, but failed to achieve this goal.

Holy Roman Emperor Frederick II and his Master of Falcons (13th Century)
© Look and Learn/Bridgeman Images

Beginning with Swiss historian Carl Jacob Christoph Burckhardt (1818–1897), many historians consider Frederick II a harbinger of the Italian Renaissance. He was a polyglot, literate in seven languages, skilled in both literary and military arts. When he fought, he invariably won. His talents were clearly equal to the giants of the Renaissance, and his reputation as the "first modern man" is not altogether accidental. In the context of the times in which he lived, however, one might accurately call him a Sicilian, a Mediterranean, or a person of the Near East.

Having grown up in Palermo, a city built by Muslims, Frederick II had no prejudices against Islam or non-Catholic Christian denominations. Fluent in Arabic and Greek, he gathered scholars, people of culture, and jurists, formulating an efficient bureaucracy, and provisioning a mobile mercenary force, despite Western Europe's devout Christianity and feudalism. He accordingly considered the Crusades ridiculous and would have no part of them. Such words and actions on his part had the effect of gaining him an increasing number of enemies in both ecclesiastical and secular circles.

In general, we might see this as the outline of a confrontation between people of the Near East and Western Europeans. Whereas the former were religiously tolerant urbanites, the latter, based in farming villages, strove to root out heresy.

While an exemplar of the peoples of the Near East, Frederick II nonetheless had to conduct himself as Holy Roman Emperor, leader of the Christian world. Even so, he aspired to unify the Italian Peninsula, taking on peoples of varying status, environment, condition, and thought, transcending belief and overcoming territorial differences. As this endeavor was misguided from the outset, it is perhaps no surprise that it ended in failure.

Ögödei to the east would have been roughly contemporary with Frederick II. Set against the remarkable state of world affairs that saw the rise of the Mongols and their dominion over Eurasia, Frederick's life—staked as it was on Sicily and Italy—was truly tragic.

Frederick II left a considerable legacy, however. He built a secular bureaucracy based in cities, entrusted warfare to mercenaries, and improved economics and literature; in short, he put his ancient Near Eastern and Mediterranean orientation into practice in Sicily and set an example for Italy. After Frederick's death, Sicily and southern Italy sank into obscurity under the feudalist rule of the French royal house. By stark contrast, the northern Italian cities inherited the mantle of Sicily and southern Italy, and it was in those cities that the flower of the Italian Renaissance would blossom.

The Context of the Renaissance

It is beyond the scope of this book to discuss the Italian Renaissance in detail. Instead, I propose to describe only its preconditions and setting. These alone should suffice to locate the position of the Renaissance in world history.

Culture can only exist where there is affluence; that is the absolute minimum necessary condition. But money alone is not sufficient. Creating a superior culture requires great skill, external stimulus, and a process of internalizing said stimulus. For that, places of thriving pluralistic intercourse and exchange are needed. The cities of northern Italy at the time had ideal conditions in this sense.

First was these cities' proximity to Rome. The hinterland of Western Europe was experiencing marked economic development. In Northern

Europe, a new commercial sphere was emerging: one with a woolen textile industry at its heart. The Vatican continued its religious exploitation of its Western European flock, chiefly in the form of donations. The resulting wealth was concentrated in Italy.

With these riches as leverage, the city-states of northern Italy— including Florence, Venice, and Genoa—connected Western Europe to the Mediterranean, which had been the center of trade with Asia, and extended trade finance on a scale stretching over the whole of Europe.

The Muslim decline in the Mediterranean, especially in terms of military power, was already evident. Their loss of Sicily to the Normans was a case in point. Even though the Muslims were able to retaliate against the Crusades in Syria and Palestine, they never recaptured control of the Mediterranean.

Port cities such as Venice and Genoa replaced Muslim control, dispatching superior fleets of ships and expanding their influence. The Muslims had by that time ceased to be rivals of the Normans. The Greeks and the Byzantines had supplanted the Muslims in that role, having obtained control of commercial rights in the eastern Mediterranean. Therefore, northern Italian port cities began to send out feelers in that direction. In the early thirteenth century, the commercial interests of these city-states had even hijacked the Crusades, as witnessed by the Fourth Crusade and its occupation of Constantinople.

Thus did control of the Mediterranean, the vital passage for Europe's trade with Asia, pass to the northern Italian city-states. The merchant ships of Genoa and Venice crisscrossed the sea as though it were their backyard, providing rare products from the East and amassing great fortunes. Florence and Venice became surpassing economic superpowers in Europe; their currencies enjoyed tremendous faith and credit as key currencies all over Europe. And it was possible for the Renaissance to happen here precisely because much of this wealth was invested in art and literature.

What Was the Renaissance?

The flower of Renaissance culture came into full bloom in economically flourishing Italy, making the country the supreme cultural force and enchanting the whole of Europe. Imitating Italy became a European pre-occupation, and the cultural level of the region was elevated as a result. Such practices as the Grand Tour, which children of modern English aristocracy would undertake with Italy as a destination, signify this fact.

Nor were Renaissance accomplishments limited to the arts. They extended as well to politics, diplomacy, and international relations. Take, for example, the hugely well-known Niccolò Machiavelli (1469–1527), founder of political science, who needless to say drew his ideas from his experiences as a Florentine diplomat. These other Renaissance achievements made it possible not only to write and theorize but also to create a system of resident ambassadors and diplomatic missions all over Italy, and eventually throughout Europe, in the latter half of the fifteenth century—roughly contemporary with Machiavelli himself.

Subsequent European civilization would have been impossible without the cultural achievements of Italy in this period. Put another way, this Italian era is named the Renaissance, and positioned as the origin of Europe and modernity, because its culture was carried on and further advanced, resulting in the modern West. The Italian Renaissance did not start out as a European Renaissance.

This point may be more easily understood when viewed in economic terms. A great deal of commercial and financial know-how, skills, and technologies relating to European economics originated in this era.

First was the expansion of *compagnie*, or corporate organizations—which diversified their business operations into such spheres as manufacturing, trading, and banking—that brought in participants outside of family connections, and created networks of branch offices. These *compagnie* are particularly well known for producing double-entry bookkeeping. Other practices established in Renaissance Italy, which we take for granted nowadays, are such negotiable securities as banknotes and money orders, as well as insurance and postal service.

It would be incorrect, of course, to conceive of the *compagnie* as an original invention of Italy or Europe, and distinct from art or politics in the sense of being influenced by such regional characteristics as language or ideology. As we saw in the Mongol era, commercial capital such as the *ortogh*, which were similar to the *compagnie*, had been greatly active in the East in earlier times, and East and West Asia had far more advanced infrastructure in place when it came to either currency and finance or traffic and communication. It would perhaps be more natural to think of such infrastructure as having arrived in Italy by way of Syria, the Eastern Roman (Byzantine) Empire, and the Mediterranean. It was little different from the route taken by classical studies and the arts and Renaissance humanism, which began with the deciphering and translation of Arabic and Greek literature. Italy's situation has been nothing more than the fortunate circumstance of having copious archives that researchers have long been able to decipher and study.

The Position of Italy in the Scheme of Things

In terms of its geography, Italy resembles a boot, though its function might be likened to that of a train-track switch or a bridge. This is because it fulfilled the geopolitical conditions of forming part of Christian Europe while also being in the ancient Near East/Mediterranean world. Italy thus propagated the advanced urban civilization of the ancient Near East/ Mediterranean world, filtered through the "Renaissance," to Christian Europe, which was feudal and based on farming districts.

From this viewpoint, both Sicily prior to Frederick II and the Renaissance-era Italian city-states were similar to the oasis city-states of Central Asia, however much they might differ in size. It is appropriate to see these various city-states as established on common principles. These points are particularly noteworthy: having highly convenient locations for grassland and maritime traffic, they were engaged in long-distance commerce; their prosperity was built by trade and finance; and they wielded leadership through economics and culture, without significant military force.

And through these attributes, each connected two disparate worlds. As Central Asia fulfilled the role of linking Islamic West Asia to non-Muslim East Asia, so too did Italy join the ancient Near East to Europe.

There are temporal parallels as well. Italy and the Renaissance were at their height in the fifteenth century, overlapping with the glory of the Timurid dynasty, which was based in Ma Wara al-Nahr (Transoxania). The flourishing of both regimes depended on emerging from the Crisis of the Fourteenth Century and surviving the plagues of the period. And both fell at the end of the fifteenth century, on the verge of the Age of Discovery.

These parallel phenomena are hardly coincidental. The Silk Road, which formed the main artery of communication and commerce through the boundary zone between the grasslands and the farms of Eurasia, had its western terminus in Syria. Such traffic and commerce were not limited to overland routes, however; where the land left off, the waterborne route of the Mediterranean picked up that artery, eventually reaching Italy. It is therefore appropriate to think of Italy as being part of the Silk Road, and rising and falling along with it.

From this perspective, by means of the Renaissance of Christian Italy, the Mediterranean can be seen as having changed at last from the stage for the ancient Near East, which it had been up to this time, to the stage for European history. The history of the Mediterranean up to the time of Frederick II had been that of an extension of the ancient Near East and a part of it. With the advent of the Renaissance, Mediterranean history became Western history, in both name and fact. And when the Mediterranean switched from the ancient Near East to Europe, the role that the Mediterranean and Italy had occupied in world historical terms drew to an end. This was the Age of Discovery.

Downfall

The Age of Discovery used to be described as a project of "geographical exploration," though it was itself a product of Italy and the Renaissance. The Genoese navigator Christopher Columbus attempted to go west to

India because he believed in the spherical earth theory propounded by Florentine scholar Paolo dal Pozzo Toscanelli (1397–1482). This led to the "discovery" of the Americas, which in turn led to Vasco da Gama's opening of the sea route from western Europe to India, and finally instigated the Age of Discovery in the sixteenth century. Hence, it was the Italians who originally undertook these "discoveries," which, in the event, were nothing but calamities, both to the indigenous peoples of the Americas and to the Italians themselves.

The reason was that Spain, which had backed Columbus' "discoveries," took possession of the Americas, extracting vast quantities of gold and silver from those lands. The Spaniards not only destroyed such Central and South American empires as the Aztecs and the Incas, and looted their precious metals, they also exploited the indigenes they conquered to mine the gold and silver, which they loaded unceasingly onto their ships.

These were extraordinary volumes of gold and silver for the time. The value of money naturally fell and prices rose, in what is known as the Price Revolution. The most severely affected was the Italian banking sector, which had controlled finance throughout Europe and even influenced the state economies of England and France. The gold coinage of Florence and Venice, which had functioned as key currencies, lost that position. The riches stored in banks in other cities also fell sharply in value. It was a blow from which there would be no recovery.

Opening the Atlantic and Indian Ocean shipping routes meant that the center of trade with Asia had moved away from the Mediterranean, as had the stage of world history. The Mediterranean soon became a provincial route. Italy's downfall was also only natural. The same was true of the ancient Near East and the Silk Road, to which Italy had been connected. The time had come for new leading players in world history.

2. From Maritime Empires to the British Empire

Spain and Portugal

The Age of Discovery in the sixteenth century afforded the opportunity to shift the linchpin of world history to Western history and to promote Europe to the role of world protagonist. That age, as is clear from Christopher Columbus' origins, originated in Italy. Needless to say, however, it was Spain and Portugal who in actuality would undertake the project, see it through, and reap the first harvest.

Spain came into possession of colossal colonies, mainly in Central and South America, rising to become the preeminent power in Europe, while Portugal monopolized trade with Asia and enjoyed economic prosperity. They were both global empires, boasting that they had divided the earth between them.

Their external scale aside, the question that instead arises is what their internal structures were like. Recall the phrase, "the ancient Near East begins at the Pyrenees." Since the Umayyad conquests, the Iberian Peninsula had been part of the Islamic world, and had long enjoyed the civilization of the Mediterranean—that is, the ancient Near East. In that sense, it was similar to Italy, whose advancement began with Sicily.

The Italian city-states linked the East with Europe, and thrived in trade and finance. Spain and Portugal had this in common with these city-states, as they were the connection between Europe and India. What differed between them were the routes and the volumes involved. By going via the oceans rather than the Mediterranean, connecting directly to places east of India, and flooding the region with great quantities of silver from the Americas, Spain and Portugal forged ever-closer ties and fostered increasingly vigorous trade between East and West, Asia and Europe.

We can see that patterns of behavior remained unchanged. This was especially true for Portugal. Even though it advanced into the Indian Ocean and managed colonies, Portugal's economic activity boiled down to acting as a middleman through the establishment of trading houses and the supply of money. It differed very little in substance from the

Muslim and Italian merchants that had previously made the Mediterranean their stage.

In this sense, neither Spain nor Portugal did anything more than supplant the Italian city-states that had controlled the Mediterranean. While they were members of the ancient Near East—that is, the Mediterranean world—their rapid progress was enabled by abandoning the Mediterranean without a second thought, or by sacrificing it. Indeed, that contradiction was also the reason that their prosperity was not sustainable.

Maritime Empires

At the time, trade between Europe and Asia was, bluntly put, the wholesale buying up of Asian products. Conversely, the only commodities transported from Europe and other parts of the West were the precious metals that were used as payment for those purchases. In addition to condiments such as pepper, there were cotton and dyes from India, and porcelain, silks, and teas from China. All of these products of Asia were rare items that could not be made with the climate and technology of contemporary Europe, making them objects of ardent desire.

Accordingly, players who were well versed in marine transport and the supply of money could hold leadership in this trade and enjoy prosperity from it. This was Mediterranean Italy in the fifteenth century and maritime Spain and Portugal in the sixteenth century. The Netherlands came next. That European economic leadership, having spread over the world, passed to the Netherlands in the seventeenth century with Amsterdam becoming the center of prosperity, was nothing more than the common sense of Western and world history.

There is a concept known as "maritime empires." It refers to nations and their spheres of influence beginning in the Age of Discovery that expanded their power to a global scale. From the sixteenth through the eighteenth centuries, these empires changed from Spain and Portugal to the Netherlands, and then to the British Empire.

Japan, as isolated islands of the Far East, and the farthest point from Europe, may be the ultimate exemplar of the sensibilities corresponding to this state of affairs. When early Portuguese traders landed in Japan, these first Westerners were received in the mid-sixteenth century, right in the middle of the Sengoku period. This was of course concurrent with the Age of Discovery. As the seventeenth century dawned, there were fewer Portuguese and more Dutch among the Westerners who arrived in Japan. To the Japanese, it simply seemed that as the Sengoku period gave way to the Edo period (1603–1867), Portugal left Japan and the Netherlands remained. Scholars of Japanese history additionally interpret this change in which Europeans remained in Japan—that is, the expulsion of the Spanish and Portuguese, leaving only the Dutch—as having been engineered solely to suit Japanese rulers, who by this time had gone from suppressing Christian missionary activity and religious practice to accomplishing *sakoku* (full national seclusion).

This would probably suffice if the only sensibilities concerned were those of Japanese and Japanese history. The same might also be true for China. But in the context of Western and world history, there is a serious problem with the notion of "maritime empires" being supplanted in this fashion.

How Western and Northern Europe Figure in the Scheme of Things

First, we should avoid treating Spain and Portugal as though they belong in the same group of "maritime empires" as the Netherlands. We can also say the same about the difference between the Netherlands and England. A given empire is supplanted by another empire because of a clear difference in gradation between what went before and what came after, and it may be more appropriate to consider each of these as occupying different dimensions.

How, then, did the Netherlands differ from what came before? The answer is clear at a glance: it differs in geographical position from Spain and Portugal. The Netherlands is located much farther north, on land that faces the North Sea, not the Mediterranean. It marks the advent of a new power, one wholly removed from the world of the ancient Near East and the Mediterranean. It also marks the beginning of a new stage in Western history.

With north-south differences in land naturally come varying climates and ecologies; lifestyles and economic matters also differ accordingly. Commensurate developments were already underway in Europe north of the Alps. Trade was flourishing on the North and Baltic Seas. The economies of Western and Northern Europe showed further increases in scale as time passed from the Renaissance to the Age of Discovery.

As Italian prosperity was linked to Italy's Mediterranean trade, so too did Spain and Portugal prosper by their maritime links. The point is that up to this time, the Mediterranean countries served as go-betweens joining Asian products with Western and Northern European markets. The advent and rise of the Netherlands signified that Europe was brushing aside these pre-existing go-betweens to connect directly with Asia.

Where Western and Northern Europe predominated, more than in any other regard, was in their extensive woodland resources. Timber was essential as both building material and as fuel, so much so that it affected the world's power relations.

The Netherlands

Take shipbuilding, for example. Wood was depleted more rapidly in the arid regions of the ancient Near East and Western Asia, with their old civilizations. And the reason that the Islamic world was unable to retaliate against the Crusaders even as it succeeded in repelling them was that it lacked adequate lumber to build ships.

Thereafter, woodland resources also dwindled noticeably in Zhongyuan in East Asia. In terms of fuel, however, East Asia was ahead of the rest of the world during the Tang-Song transition in adopting coal and coke as fuel, thereby achieving an energy revolution. This development also contributed significantly to the Mongol conquest of Eurasia. Moreover, in terms of materials, by developing the adjacent territory of Jiangnan, Zhongyuan was able to draw upon lush mountain forests. This woodland resources factor also explains why the relative power balance in Asia, in which West Asia had long held superiority over East Asia, was inverted around the tenth century.

That being so, then the next region after West Asia where woodlands were depleted was the Mediterranean world linked to the ancient Near East. This was why the Italian maritime states were ultimately unable to leave the Mediterranean and lost their leading roles in the Age of Discovery to Spain and Portugal.

By contrast, the Netherlands utilized the abundant resources of Northern and Western Europe to steadily increase its presence in seaborne commerce, drawing even with and eventually surpassing Spain and Portugal. Having already established itself in trade on the North and Baltic Seas, the Netherlands occupied an advantageous position connected to the open ocean. This position was so advantageous that by the mid-seventeenth century, the Netherlands owned two-thirds of all the ships in Europe.

Western and Northern Europe were also superior to Spain and Portugal in crop yields and manufacturing, specifically in grains and woolen textiles. More than anything else, the woolen textile industry that had made great strides in Flanders, adjacent to the Netherlands, was on the verge of becoming a key European industry. And it was tied to finance and commerce through the regional markets of Western and Northern Europe.

The central node of these markets was Antwerp, gateway to Flanders. Its resources and functions moved to the Netherlands, a country with harbors suited to international trade, which had gained independence from Spain. The Netherlands became active on the world stage not only because it possessed hitherto unsurpassed seaborne transport capability but also because it was directly connected to the markets of Western and Northern Europe, which had manufacturing and production capability unlike anything before. This was a structure unlike the Mediterranean transit trade that had thriven solely on finance and seaborne transport.

The Atlantic Economic Sphere

As hegemony over trade and economy on a global scale thus shifted, what might be termed an Atlantic revolution was well underway. An economic sphere was coming together that would integrate the Atlantic coasts of Western Europe, the Americas, and Africa.

Fig. 29. The Atlantic Triangle Trade (c. 18th Century)
Reproduced from Kawakita Minoru, *Sato no sekaishi* [A World History of Sugar] (Tokyo: Iwanami Shoten, 1996).

Figure 29 depicts the Atlantic Triangle Trade established in the eighteenth century. Comparing this configuration with, for example, Figure 27 (p. 152), reveals at a glance the state of the transition to English leadership.

In the Americas, which had initially served only to supply silver, colonization and development advanced. These continents were the source for the primary products that Europe consumed, including sugar and cotton. Europe and the Americas formed a steadily closer economic relationship.

By being inseparably bound to Asian trade, this economic sphere eventually rose to greater superiority than the Asian economies, forming the prototype for the capitalist world economy that has been driven continuously to this day. It was England that fulfilled the central role in this conversion.

Historical and economic-historical studies of the world alike have brought all their resources to bear in elucidating and describing the historical evidence and the image of the history of the time. Wallerstein's world-systems theory is an exemplar of these efforts, and in Japan as well, Kawakita Minoru has the enduring achievement of having long expounded and advanced this doctrine. For example, his book *Sato no sekaishi* (A World History of Sugar) skillfully depicts an image of world economic history at this highwater mark for the world, using nontechnical Japanese that can be understood even by high school students.

Quantitative Expansion

The situation becomes easier to understand if we consider that initially, both the Netherlands and England had nearly the same relations with Asia in their broad trade structures, even having experienced such great transitions as I have described. Nor was the Netherlands inferior to England in terms of power relations in the early half of the seventeenth century. The example of Japan, in which Dutch traders remained even as the country entered *sakoku*, makes clear the status of the Netherlands vis-à-vis England at this time.

Until the early half of the eighteenth century, the particulars remained essentially like those of the period of Dutch leadership. Of course, England and the Netherlands had different and competing spheres of influence and scopes of activity in Asia and trafficked in different items as well. Ultimately, however, there was no reason to prefer one over the other when it came to bringing Asian products to Europe.

That being the case, what changed when the Netherlands was supplanted by England? In a word: volume. Heretofore unheard-of quantitative increases kept on growing.

The Age of Discovery and the discovery of the Americas brought about the Price Revolution and caused the decline of the Mediterranean due to unprecedented silver production. This was the beginning of the quantitative expansion. However, trade by Spain and Portugal, which commanded the oceans, amounted to nothing more than taking silver to Asia and bringing back Asian products. Their connections to continuously expanding European domestic industry and commerce were meager.

The Netherlands achieved such connections, took leadership in Asian trade from Portugal, and managed even greater prosperity than Portugal.

Yet for all that, there was nothing to distinguish the nature and structure of Dutch trade with Asia from that of the Portuguese.

Initially, England was no different in this regard. Where England distinguished itself was in its even more rapid quantitative expansion and the internal reformation that this brought about.

The Advent of Great Britain

Portugal and the Netherlands are both small countries with little land area. Nevertheless, they dominated Western trade with Asia, achieved great prosperity, and their merchants were highly active. Though both were respectively superior in maritime shipping, neither had naval power commensurate with their waterborne transport capacity. There were no particularly strong ties between their regimes and their merchants. Or rather, the regimes themselves were not strong governments, which they had in common with the Italian city-states of ancient Near East origin. Spain, which was a mighty power, conversely had little to no presence in Asian trade.

It seems that the difference that led to the switch from the Netherlands to England lies here. England aspired to be a great power, politically and militarily. Or perhaps it would be more apt to say that England ended up becoming such a great power. In all events, beginning with the defeat of the Spanish Armada in the late sixteenth century and continuing through its battles with France in what is sometimes called the Second Hundred Years' War, England rose to become one of the preeminent great powers of Europe in the latter half of the eighteenth century, influencing international politics on the European continent.

At the same time, England battled the Netherlands for commercial rights, securing Atlantic economic leadership for itself and becoming the "maritime empire" that replaced the Netherlands. In the two hundred years prior to the late eighteenth century, the amount of shipping controlled by the English reached some one million fifty thousand tons, an increase of over two hundredfold.

England was not like Portugal or the Netherlands, however. It was not simply a power in terms of shipping and commerce but was also a naval power, with political and military influence. These factors would also lead to the Industrial Revolution.

In terms of the British Empire that was to come, this all may seem only to be expected. On further consideration, however, we realize that never before had there been such a country as this. It was without precedent in all of recorded history. And this fact has tremendous meaning in terms of world history.

England's Dawn

How did England get this way? To answer this question, it seems that we must go back to the country's very founding.

England's beginnings as a unified country date back to the Norman Conquest in the latter half of the eleventh century, a time when a new social configuration and international order had taken root in East Asia following the economic advancement of the Tang-Song transition. Guillaume, Duke of Normandy, conquered England and ascended its throne as William I (1027–1087).

The region of Normandy was the part of present-day France that faces Britain. As its name suggests, it was occupied by the Normans, who descended from Northern Europe and became French feudal lords. As it was also the home of the people who built the Norman kingdom of Sicily that was introduced in the previous sections, Normandy can be thought of as the base for northern and southern conquests alike.

From then on until the Hundred Years' War, England held lands across the English Channel in France as well as at home. Or rather, it would be more accurate to say that, as a vassal of the French king reigned in England, England was a possession of France. In fact, taxes collected from English lords were used in the defense and operation of French domains.

In any event, rulers from William I onward had to govern lands in both England and France and had to keep reliable control over influential lords. Thus, they went back and forth across the English Channel, going to all of their lands to rule there directly. It is said that William made

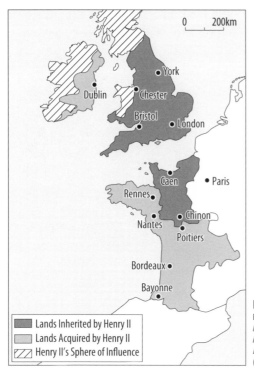

Fig. 30. The Angevin Empire

Reproduced from Kimizuka Naotaka, *Monogatari Igirisu no rekishi (Jo): Kodai Buriten-to kara Erizabesu issei made* [History of Great Britain (Part 1): From Ancient Britain to the Age of Queen Elizabeth I] (Tokyo: Chuokoron Shinsha, 2015).

Lands Inherited by Henry II
Lands Acquired by Henry II
Henry II's Sphere of Influence

nine round-trip channel crossings over the approximately twenty years of his reign.

The largest such domain possessed by an English king occurred during the mid-twelfth century reign of Henry II (1133–1189). At the time, he was lord of the greatest dominion in Western Europe. Including the western half of modern-day France, his rule extended from the Scottish border to the Pyrenees. This territory was commonly referred to as the "Angevin Empire" after Henry's Angevin heritage.

As territory expanded, so too did the

King Henry II
© National Portrait Gallery, London

need for continental defense. While securing support in England, the king had to spend extended periods in France to attend to governing there. Henry himself spent nearly two-thirds of his thirty-five-year reign in France, and died there.

This situation was quite unnatural. This was revealed in the reign of Henry's son, John, king of England, known as John Lackland (1167–1216), as well as in the Hundred Years' War in the century after John's reign. John lost nearly all of England's possessions on the continent, and was forced to accept the Magna Carta in order to retain the support of English lords who opposed John's taxation on their produce and con-

King John of England
Photo from Heritage Image Partnership Ltd./Alamy Stock Photo

scription of their peasants into his armies. As a result, policy decisions and exercise of power by the king would be possible only if they accorded with the opinion of all free men in England and the due process of law. This marked the beginning of rule of law and the parliamentary system.

This situation became fixed with England's defeat in the Hundred Years' War in the mid-fifteenth century. Consolidated only in the island of Britain at last, England started over.

Rule of Law, Anglo-Saxon Style

I have taken this space to describe England's early history in detail up to the time of John Lackland because he was a contemporary of Genghis Khan. The fall of the "Angevin Empire" was nearly the polar opposite of the conquests of the Mongol Empire. The Angevin fall was not its ruin, however. Instead, it led to the birth of a system unprecedented in history. In this way, too, England was the opposite of the Mongols, in that the latter were the ultimate exponent of the history of Asia before them.

The first thing to know is that England was a small, backward country.

It got its start as a nation no earlier than the time of the Tang-Song transition, and by the time of the Renaissance at the latest. Moreover, even in its "Angevin Empire" period it was only somewhat larger than modern-day Japan; compared to the many Asian regimes culminating in the Mongol Empire, it was only ever a very small-scale place. And the "Angevin Empire" would get even smaller, reduced to only England itself.

It was the condition of English royal authority to make circuits of all of its narrow domains and solicit their cooperation in warfare and taxation. To systematize these procedures, the parliamentary system was born, which promulgated laws that bound both the monarch and his subjects: the high ruled the low, and the low constrained the high. This marked the beginning of a bi-directional system of government, vertically integrating high and low, rulers and ruled.

David Hume (1711–1776) consistently expounded the significance of this development of English history. He called it the replacement of "government of will" with "government of law" (Meinecke, *Die Entstehung des Historismus*). This comment, which is apt to be taken to simply mean different forms of government, actually refers to the overall configuration of society, a system that was born of the particular form taken by English feudalism.

Real-world implementations of government of law are seen in the parliamentary system in terms of legislation, and in the court system in terms of the judiciary. Whether in legislatures, where rulers meet the ruled, or in the courts, where defendants confront plaintiffs, these are clearly uniform, bi-directional systems. Conversely, the concept of rule of law could also be termed the backbone upon which these systems were formed.

A Coherent Nation

Such systems are of course not limited to legislation or the judiciary. They also apply to public finance and banking. England was the first country to issue government debt and establish a central bank. Essentially, government debt is a system in which government authority, in addition to taxes that it has secured, borrows money from the private sector, and repays said money to the private sector in turn. With this bi-directional switch between the issuer and receiver of capital, bonds—which are the lending securities—become instruments for investment. Banks operate on the same principle. As the same bank had debt in the form of deposits, it performed the functions of making loans on the one hand and issuing banknotes—that is, paper money—on the other hand, with reserve funds comprising a portion of deposits backing such issuances.

In other words, a system of credit was established and expanded, eventually giving rise to private-sector corporations. And this system required control by government authority; that is, rule of law, such that sanctions could be imposed against malfeasance.

This system of public finance and banking arose from the strains of supporting a military. Since the early times of William I and Henry II, England had been plagued by constant shortages of war funds. To raise such monies, rounds were made of the domains, a legislature created, and a bank established. These acts necessitated rule of law and the accompanying exercise of sanctions, as well as the concentration and centralization of armed force and violence.

At the same time, the Military Revolution took place, leading to the formation of a "fiscal-military state." Beginning with the invention of firearms, weapon performance and technology steadily improved and the organization of armed forces also changed, rapidly strengthening the government's monopoly on violence. These changes also accompanied an ever-growing public finance which, through integrated bi-directional systems, affected not only government authority but also civil society, in the form of expanded credit and the movements of colossal amounts of money (Brewer, *The Sinews of Power: War, Money, and the English State, 1688–1783*).

Thus, politics, the military, public finance, and banking were tightly bound together within tiny England. By vertical integration and the union of monarchs and subjects, a coherent nation was established. This was the driving force behind the quantitative expansion of the "Atlantic economic sphere," and the foundation for the Industrial Revolution and capitalism.

To this foundation were added Flanders-style woolen textile manufacturing and Dutch-style shipping and commerce. It could be said that
these were imitated and replaced. England had never had any noteworthy intrinsic industry of its own. England's development and supremacy,
whether in woolen textiles or shipping, were achieved through the integration of public finance and banking, as well as through the government
policy of mercantilism.

At last, England triumphed in the Anglo-Dutch Wars that began in the
mid-seventeenth century, wresting the position of maritime empire from
the Netherlands in addition to its woolen textile and shipping industries.
In the long ministry that was Sir Robert Walpole's (1676–1745) time of leadership in the Commons in the early half of the eighteenth century, England
had finally become an acknowledged superpower: the British Empire.

3. Imperialism and Empires East and West

The Industrial Revolution

In the early half of the eighteenth century, British control of European
economic leadership displaced that of the Netherlands. Initially, the overall global configuration was not significantly different from the period of
Dutch control. In essence, Britain formed the Atlantic economic sphere, and
used the wealth acquired from this sphere to purchase products from Asia,
carrying on exactly as its predecessors had since the Age of Discovery.

The major changes concerned the quantities of and means for making the wealth that was made within the Atlantic economic sphere. Over
some two hundred years since the sixteenth century, the index illustrat-
ing this transformation could be said to trace the rise and decline of the
maritime empires—that is, the supplanting of Spain and Portugal by the
Netherlands, and then of the Netherlands by Britain.

By way of these changes, Britain ultimately became the engine of
the Atlantic economic sphere. Having been the first country to achieve

political and economic integration, Britain's output as economic engine was unheard-of, and the Atlantic economic sphere further enlarged its own driving force.

In other words, in the eighteenth century, the West was able to buy up Asian products in unprecedented quantities. Nor was such buying limited to such established luxuries as spices, perfumes, silks, and porcelain. Indian cotton and Chinese tea became even more important than these, for clothing and food were integral to people's daily lives. Therefore, having once matched popular preferences, it was possible to sustain an expansion of demand and consumption. And as the Atlantic economic sphere, with its continuing growth and advancement, was buying up these goods, such demand and consumption would increase even more, never declining.

As trade with Asia continued only in the sense of laying in Asian products, there was likely no substantive difference between the British period and the Dutch period, even with variation in the quantities involved. During this period of trade, the best of the modern European world economy emerged, marking the start of a new era: the Industrial Revolution.

What was this revolution? It can be debated in many ways, both in definition and impact: industrialization, mechanization, mass production, capitalism, labor problems, and the like. Seen, however, from its intrinsic objective, on the scale of global and world history, the point of the Industrial Revolution was for Europe to catch up with Asian industry and provide substitutes for imports of Asian products. The principal target was Indian cotton.

As a result of Britain's Asian trade, Indian cotton dominated Western markets. This led to a demand to produce such cotton domestically, which was then researched and actually achieved. Europe's ability to catch up was prodigious. The result was the Manchester cotton industry: mass production by mechanized industry.

The British Empire and the Marshaling of Revolution

Mechanization could only work with the invention of the steam engine,

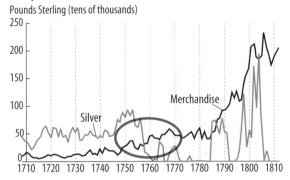

1. Exports from Britain to Asia (1708–1811)

Pounds Sterling (tens of thousands)

2. Movement of Cotton (1771–1845)

Pounds Sterling (tens of thousands)

Fig. 31. East-West Trade
Adapted from Matsui Toru, *Sekai shijo no keisei* [Formation of a World Market] (Tokyo: Iwanami Shoten, 1991), 217, 225.

the energy source that would replace manpower. As Europe could not be industrialized without machines, technological innovations born of scientific revolutions came into play. Industrialization was thereby achieved, making mass production possible.

Once things are made, they must be sold. Production and manufacture are predicated on purchase and consumption; otherwise, only costs and inventory remain. Mass production, for which tremendous infrastructure investment and labor input are indispensable, requires trade and commerce. Markets are essential to recovering outlays, expansion, and reproduction. These are among the core principles of capitalism.

As cotton products overflowed the Atlantic economic sphere, it became necessary to find other markets in which to sell them. Military strength and political power were mobilized to this end. In concrete terms, a revolution in military affairs was brought to bear to make the already subordinate India into a market.

In other words, having militarily conquered India and politically controlled it as a colony, Britain used "non-economic compulsion" to change India's economic conditions into markets for British industrial products. Through manipulations of such factors as tariffs and exchange rates, Britain accomplished "the draining away of wealth" from India. Thus, as shown in Figure 31, the West, which had been nothing more than a one-sided buyer of Asian products, succeeded in reversing its position. At this point, the weight of world history shifted decisively from Asia to Europe.

For India, this historical process was the worst possible disaster. It was also disastrous for China, as these events would eventually lead to the introduction of opium from India as well as the resulting Opium Wars. This was the formation of what is called in textbooks the "triangle trade" among the Atlantic economic sphere, India, and China. Thus, the modern world economy—the capitalist world—was predicated on Asian calamities. These are also the phenomena that signify the prosperity of the British Empire.

The Modern World Economy and Its Core

Through the century of the Industrial Revolution, the British Empire and the modern West gained the upper hand over Asia, subordinating it, and at last dominated the world. Its supremacy, however, was neither solely industrial nor purely economic.

To secure such economic power, Europe needed scientific revolutions that gave rise to energy sources surpassing manpower or horsepower by far, as well as the Military Revolution in which command of firepower crushed other political forces. This economic power was the fruit of marshaling and organically combining many revolutions.

All of these revolutions required funds—that is, capital. Using machinery and firearms to conduct revolution demanded tremendous amounts of money. And the key to procuring such funds was credit. As per

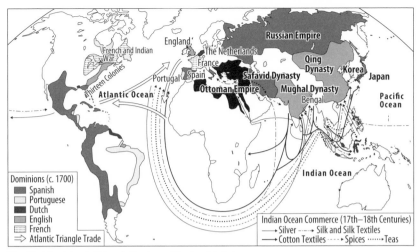

Fig. 32. The Atlantic Triangle Trade and Trade with Asia

History of Economic Analysis, by economist and sociologist Joseph Alois Schumpeter (1883–1950), credit provides an intrinsic part of capitalism.

Credit can take a variety of forms. One friend picking up the tab for another constitutes credit, however familiar and small it might be. At the opposite extreme are banks and corporations that collect money from large numbers of people and companies in the form of deposits and investments. These are instances of extensive large-scale credit. In either case, there is a trustworthy party from whom repayment can be expected, which facilitates lending. This provides the key to loans and the settlement of transactions.

Variations in scope aside, credit as a concept is uniform and unchanging in substance. However, ways of establishing credit other than by small-scale lending are necessary to amassing large capital.

The Expansion of Credit and the Emergence of Investing

Among acquaintances, oral agreements are sufficient for the lending of small sums; nothing more elaborate in the way of credit is needed. Put another way, credit of this kind is only adequate for people close to oneself and for amounts of money that individuals can personally dispose of. Once this range is exceeded, early repayments and high interest rates are inevitable if bad debts are to be avoided. These measures complicate the gathering and long-term management of large sums of capital.

If large-scale credit is to be created, lending must be systematized so as to eliminate such limitations. Rules are required to guarantee that even if one lends money to strangers beyond the scope of one's personal recognizance, then such money will be repaid.

One simple example of such rules is the demand for collateral. Other methods include regulations on business, such as accounting audits and bankruptcy proceedings to avoid the risk that invested capital will be misappropriated or irrecoverable.

Implementing any of these measures requires far-reaching financial management and market regulation, or in less abstract terms, legal sanctions on misconduct and breach of trust related to lending and the settlement of accounts. And such sanctions are provided by political bodies that have monopolies on legislation and violence. This means that political authority must be integrated with social economy: the core of the system is found in such political authority. Its existence enables the collection of diffuse idle funds from large numbers of people and the formation and mobilization of such funds as large capital.

The exemplar of such large capital formation was the joint-stock company that developed in modern Europe. Although no different in essence from the borrowing and lending of money, moving money around ceases to be called making loans when it is carried out through systems of negotiable securities known as stocks and bonds. It has become investment. Even if the strict form of a joint-stock company was not adopted, Western enterprises commenced and conducted business in this way to varying degrees, thereby standing out from the rest of the contemporary world in terms of abundance of funds and scale of business.

Nor was this state of affairs confined to the private sector. Public finances were similar targets for investment. Through the issuance of public debt and government bonds that began in England, it became possible to organize such public finances on a large scale, and these became inseparably intertwined with private-sector banking. The driving force behind this was the integrated structure of authority with society, of politics with economy—that is, of the public and private sectors.

Imperialism and the Present Age

The wellspring of Western powers' military forces, supreme in the world in the eighteenth and nineteenth centuries, lay in the mobilization and application of firepower and energy, as well as in technological innovation. None of these would have come to fruition, however, without colossal amounts of money, which were underpinned by public finance and banking that had become gigantic under the system of public-private sector integration.

Turning to Western corporations, these by no means procured capital simply through the same system of credit that the public sector used. In accordance with the selection through competition and "extended reproduction" that are the logic of capitalism, the activities of these enterprises, which were deployed on global scales, were in step with political and military affairs. The exemplar in this regard is armed conquest and colonial administration as experienced by India and Southeast Asia.

The Western powers used their overwhelming military power to wage war and intimidate the Qing dynasty, the Ottoman Empire, and other East and West Asian regimes, thereby securing economic interests. What became known as "gunboat policy" or "gunboat diplomacy" became an indispensable premise for and backing of foreign economic activity. In no time at all, such activity progressed to imperialism, which Vladimir Lenin (1870–1924) would call "the highest stage of capitalism."

Subsequent history is that of modern and current times, in which imperialism has blanketed the Earth, unifying the world. This past is directly connected with the author's own people, the Japanese. Japan appears as one of the key players; there is no need to belabor the point. Though the crucial question remains of how to interpret and evaluate it, the historical record is unequivocal in big-picture terms.

The twentieth century was a gory period in which the Western powers, having become imperialist, came into conflict among themselves even as they dominated the world: witness the two World Wars. Asia, Africa, and any other regions outside the powers were compelled without exception into unilateral subordination to one degree or another.

Of course, there has been no small amount of resistance to such submission, nor has bloodshed been spared. The overall trend of twentieth-century Asian history has been the eventual arrival at the realization that the only way to escape such circumstances of subjugation and bloody resistance has been to become Westernized, militarily, politically, and economically. Voluntary Westernization on the part of non-Western states has maintained the present-day global social order. And yet this movement harbors a great contradiction within itself.

Great Divergence, Great Convergence

It was in the modern era—beginning in the nineteenth century—that a sharp distinction was made between West and non-West, and relations between these became a case of the former subordinating the latter. Global history calls this the "Great Divergence." Therefore, the remarkable economic growth and prominence that non-Western states have begun to show in recent times would instead, in a reversal of the "divergence," represent a "Great Convergence," in which these states have grown closer to the advanced Western states.

Whether one speaks of "divergence" or "convergence," the foundational premise is that originally these were the same. That is, there was no fundamental difference between the West and the non-West; they were homogeneous. Having been sundered in modern times, in the present day they are in the process of being reunited. The rise of emerging nations that had been subordinated, such as India and China, is given as evidence.

This is the shape of world history as rendered by the California School, and which forms the accepted wisdom the world over. Although it is clear and easily understood, there are rudimentary questions that cannot be dismissed: Is it really appropriate to declare the era when West and non-West "diverged" to be the eighteenth-century and England's Industrial Revolution? Has there really been a "divergence" at all?

It seems an incontrovertible fact that Asia and the West were separated in the modern era. If, however, they were different, far removed from one another, to begin with, then this cannot be termed a "divergence." Therefore, a "Great Convergence," which is predicated on the "Great Divergence," is itself logically impossible as well.

In quantitative terms, the core regions of East Asia and Western Europe were at the same economic level—that is, homogeneous—up until the eighteenth century. Then Britain took off, having achieved the Industrial Revolution by utilizing coal and coke, and East and West diverged, according to the Pomeranz "Great Divergence" thesis.

Yet even if East and West were numerically similar, it does not necessarily follow that they were also alike in substance and character. The East, too, had undergone an energy revolution in the use of coal as a fuel resource in the Tang-Song transition. The West had industrialized while the East had not: same cause, yet different results. It becomes increasingly difficult to say that East and West were homogeneous. The observation is much too crude.

"The European Miracle"

Comparative history is hard, because comparisons can be made only if conditions are the same. How are we to spot the differences? Homogeneity is inconceivable with the historical data available to us. Hence, hypotheses and postulates are essential if we are to formulate a common set of conditions. This is even more true when quantifying these conditions.

In the case of the "Great Divergence" concept, Pomeranz decided that East and West could be compared by quantitative approximation. While there is considerable doubt about how such quantitative measurements should be made, even before that objection could be raised, there was little effort put into examining East-West structural conditions. Whereas Britain and Europe fall into the category of Western history, and thus there are no mistakes in terms of what is generally known about them, interpreting the historical record of East Asia is dubious through and through. Mistakes in conditions or hypotheses make any sort of comparison impossible, even before numerical values are taken into account. For this reason, talk of "divergence" is hard to accept.

As described herein, it should be clear that the presence of modern world economics could only have emerged in the West, where the system of a country ruled by law was created, with Britain being the first of these. In this structure, trade and finance were integrated with production, and all of these were further integrated with politics and the military. And at the core was rule of law, which unified rulers and ruled, and public and private sectors. Such a structure was necessary for a country to grow to immense scale and conquer the world. And it derived from a history unique to Britain and Europe. It could not have happened in any other realm.

In the book *The European Miracle* (Jones, *The European Miracle: Environments, Economies and Geopolitics in the History of Europe and Asia*), it is clear that the author's use of "miracle" in the title is meant to indicate that the modern era, which resulted from the rise of Europe, could only have happened in Europe. As we are living in the world created by this "miracle," we are prone to take it for granted. Yet Asia, which occupies the majority of the world and has long been the principal player in world history, did not possess the conditions for making such a "miracle" happen.

Empires in the East and Rule of Law

The foundations of and keys to quantitative expansion of production and commerce, as well as the resulting Industrial Revolution, were trust in contracts and protection of property, as these achieved the formation of capital. Theoretical economist Sir John Richard Hicks (1904–1989) declared that legal systems were necessary to bring these about, and that they were impossible in traditional societies (Hicks, *A Theory of Economic History*). We may take "traditional societies" to mean those prior to the Netherlands in Western history, and the whole of Asia in Eastern history. That is, "traditional societies" have a multipolar structure in which authority is separate from the people, as politics is separate from the economy, and legal systems are not established.

In terms of eighteenth-century China, as referred to by Pomeranz in *The Great Divergence*, capital was generally much smaller there than in the West. Even monopolistic commercial capital, supposedly the most affluent of all, struggled continuously with a shortage of funds. This state of affairs would have been immediately evident to compradors engaged in trade with England. Commercial traders were not the only ones so afflicted, however.

The lack of legal systems meant that credit could be extended only among personal networks, inherently restricting those with whom moneylending could be carried out. While there might be loans and banking, the concept of enterprise investment was unthinkable. This too was due to the structure in which public and private sectors, politics and economy, were not integrated.

Why, then, was there no structure in Asia in which authority and the people, politics and economy, were integrated? The reason is that different organizations were responsible for each of these.

As has been discussed at length in this book, the setting of Asian history emerged from a combination of multipolar zones of arid and humid, grassland and farmland, nomadic and settled. Historical processes have developed as negotiation, interaction, alliance, confrontation, and conflict between each of these. These are the dynamics of Asian history.

Of these, the nomadic grassland regions had military supremacy, while the settled farmlands were economically superior. Commerce and finance quickly developed at the boundary between these zones, fulfilling the role of connecting them to one another. Although they differed in language, faith, and custom, they were in a relationship of complementary functions. This allowed rapid formation of large political forces provided that these partnerships operated harmoniously. The greatest of these was the Mongol Empire.

Under the internal configuration of Asian history that culminated in the structure of the Mongol Empire, various multipolar bodies accordingly had respective responsibility for politics and economy. Therefore, the whole could not be reduced to a single integrated body, nor could there be a legal system that governed over all. In the strictest sense, rule of law did not operate over an integrated public and private sector. The so-called post-Mongol regimes of the Ottoman Empire and the Mughal and Qing dynasties were of similar multipolar structures, and thus followed the same process.

By way of caution, let me add that the presence or absence of such rule of law is the product of the conditions of the natural environments in which people live, and the configuration of the political societies that arose historically on the basis of those conditions. By no means is this a question of relative merit, nor can this be treated as an issue for evaluating right or wrong based on present-day world standards.

Empires in the West and the Middle Ages

Europe was practically cut off from the Asian historical staging configuration and dynamics as described here. In essence, it had a uniform structure, one that lacked the nomadic grassland zone. The history of early Europe is thus one in which authority and the people alike concentrated their efforts on increased agricultural productivity.

Europe at the time of the Mongol Empire comprised the "Angevin Empire," as described previously. Though both were called "empire," they were utterly unlike one another in external aspect and in internal nature. Henry II, who ruled the so-called Angevin Empire, was the greatest lord of twelfth-century Europe. Yet the area of his domain was on a par with present-day Japan, a fraction the size of the Mongol Empire. What do such isolated size differences signify?

That the king of England diligently traveled throughout his "empire" in order to secure his rule has already been explained. Moreover, this process was not limited to England. Feudal European lords did the same thing in their own domains to one degree or another. This closeness between rulers and those they ruled was characteristic of the feudal system that defined the "Middle Ages" in Europe. However large the various countries of Europe were, the land area, the scale, of these countries was not so great as to make such travel by their nobles impractical. It would have been out of the question with either the Mongol Empire of the same period or any of the Asian entities that adopted the same structure as the Mongols in controlling vast areas.

Feudalism, which brought together high and low, rulers and ruled, eventually integrated the public and private sectors in England. While unique to England, it was easily imitated in Europe, as feudalism was a condition that applied in general across the continent.

Additionally, the rule of law undergirding this system was a secularized adaptation of the doctrines, precepts, and taboos of Christianity, which bound everyone, irrespective of whether they were ruler or ruled, ecclesiastic or laity. Europe, which had once been uniformly Christian and which achieved separation of church and state, amassed the most suitable conditions for this system to take root.

Beginning with the Renaissance, the West borrowed commerce and finance that had originated in Asia, and advanced and modified them, thereby engineering a string of revolutions. We might say that this process is ongoing even now.

Put another way, feudalism, Christianity, and separation of church and state were necessary for the establishment of the modern world economy. If we term feudalism and Christianity "the Middle Ages," then modernity would have been impossible where the prerequisite of "the Middle Ages" was absent. And there was no "Middle Age" in Asian history.

Therefore, East and West did not "diverge." They differed from the outset. If one is still determined to call this a "divergence," then one should say that such a "divergence" began either long before the Middle Ages, or else was rooted in initial ecological conditions.

A VIEW OF JAPANESE AND WORLD HISTORY

"The Middle Ages" and "the Modern Era"

The Middle Ages in Europe used to be called the Dark Ages. This historical view originated in the Renaissance. From the standpoint of that period and later times, the preceding period was pervaded with the absurdities of Christianity, a time when people were unenlightened, dehumanized, and lacking in discernment. The choice of the word "renaissance" refers to a "restoration" of the lost classics of bygone times, proof that this period is seen as a rejection of a status quo of "darkness."

"Middle Ages" (*moyen âge* in French) means an in-between time, a transitional era. Ancient times, and the "modern age" that has "re-created" and inherited those ancient times, are the periods that have value, significance, and substance. A "Middle Age" is nothing more nor less than an interruption—an interregnum—between these other periods. Such a negative evaluation demands rejection.

It was the likes of Hegel in philosophy and Marx in economics who proactively attached such meaning to "darkness" in this context. This meaning lay in their describing the Dark Ages as a period in which Christian civilization was founded and developed, switching to, and elevating, a social economy centered on feudal production. To be sure, objectively speaking, Europe would not be Europe, nor would there be a "modern era," without Christianity and feudalism.

There is no doubt that Western modernity inherited the Middle Ages in terms of social organization, behavior pattern, structures, and systems, even as it rejected the Middle Ages as ideology, awareness, and worldview. It is this combination of medieval interregnum and continuity that gave impetus to the birth of the modern era.

Thus, beyond a doubt, what made Europe the continent that it became lay in the Middle Ages itself. It is important that Hegel and Marx alike treated this period as one of "progress," not as an interregnum.

The Modern Era and Historical Studies

The ethos of the Renaissance lay in striving to recover the respect for humanity that had been inhibited and ruptured by adversity and religion. In scholarly terms, this meant a conversion from theology to the study of human beings—that is, humanism. At the time, there was no awareness beyond going from interregnum to renewal and conversion. In the nineteenth century, however, the perception, the concept, of progress took root. The idea was one of advancing from the Middle Ages to a different reality—the modern era.

From the Renaissance to that later time, the West underwent a series of revolutions: commercial, military, scientific, industrial, and bourgeois. It was a marvelous transformation. Through this process, Europe accomplished amazing progress, eventually dominating the world. These are facts beyond doubt; moreover, the West still retains its grip on the hegemony it secured back then. More than anything, the concept of "globalism," which encompasses the modern world, attests to this situation.

It would be only natural for Europeans in previous centuries to have been enraptured by this state of affairs. Bear in mind that such sentiments were not simply conceit on their part. They were attempting to build a theory that would explain and justify the eminence they had attained, and use it to persuade themselves and others of its correctness. To fulfill this role, numerous academic and scientific disciplines were founded and systematized.

Eurocentrism is thus embedded in the substance of all manner of academic studies. It will not do for modern academia to be indifferent and insensible to this.

At the time, there was a particular need for a study, a logic, that could explain the course of human progress and advancement that had seized the modern era. The recovery and renewal of humanity alone was no longer sufficient. Then a reason was found for humanism to give birth to modern historical studies: historical studies had, above all, the task of perceiving this advancement into the modern era.

Therefore, historical studies are incomplete without the Middle Ages and the modern era styled as being the advancement from the Middle Ages. In other and more direct words, history with progress and advancement cannot exist where a Middle Ages aspect is absent.

There was no medieval period in Asian history like Europe's. That being so, progress and advancement were not possible, nor could there be history. Hence, the theory of Asian stagnation that Hegel and Marx promulgated was the inevitable logical conclusion of the mindset that gave rise to modern historical studies.

The Existence of a Middle Age: China and Japan

In the 1850s, when he was living in London, Marx indicated that he had hopes for China, far to the east. This was because China had opened its ports as a result of the Opium War that began with the outbreak of hostilities in 1840. Marx predicted that the industrial products of English capitalism would flow into China, causing unrest in its society that would eventually lead to revolution. He foresaw that such a revolution would drastically shrink the Chinese market, causing a depression in England, striking a blow at the capitalists, and resulting in revolutions happening next in Europe.

Contrary to his expectations, however, English exports to China did not increase. The reason that Marx found for this, in an investigative report by an English diplomat, was the subsistence socioeconomic structure, in which agriculture and domestic industry were solidly connected to cheap labor, forming a barrier to the import of industrial products; in other words, agriculture and industry remained undifferentiated.

Given these conditions, struggles or revolutions by class-differentiated workers (the proletariat) were inconceivable. For Marx and his associates, China at the time accordingly remained in the category of "stagnant" Asia.

China, however, was not the only part of East Asia that Marx showed interest in: Japan was also in his sights.

The appearance of late Edo-period Japan—i.e., the mid-nineteenth century—in *Das Kapital* is a perennially well-known story among Japanese. Marx wrote that "Japan, with its purely feudal organisation of landed property and its developed *petite culture*, gives a much truer picture of the European middle ages than all our history books." Although there are various hypotheses about what source materials Marx used as reference in this regard, it is beyond the scope of this book to examine them. Suffice to say that Marx found commonalities between Japan and Europe in the concepts of "feudalism" and the "middle ages."

Marx himself never saw China or Japan in person. He merely imagined their societies, based on fragmentary documents and travelogues. Nonetheless, his insights were rather shrewd. His differentiation between China and Japan from their respective social structures indicates a distinctly different intellect from that of other contemporary and later Westerners, who carelessly tend to see the two as indistinguishable from one another.

Of course, the notion that China and Asia as a whole had stagnated was baseless discrimination. Because of the difficulties in developing sophisticated commerce and finance and in amassing large-scale capital, the economic structure was one of small, isolated occupations and business management. This situation merely appeared to be stagnation to Europeans, given the significant progress they were making at the time. The transition to domestic production of goods originally from Asia, which had been born there of such "stagnant" socioeconomic structures, was finally achieved in this era, when contemporary Europe applied "progressive" methods to do so.

The modern era, which Europe created through progress, was a miracle that could only have happened in Europe. And the medieval period that provides the origin and the principal for this miracle was also unique to the West. The trajectory of the gestation and birth of this progress and miracle has become an immovable point of reference in scholarly thought. From this viewpoint, the history of Asia, which occupies the greater part of Eurasia, only has significance if it is "stagnant."

The Japanese, Historical Studies, and Japanese History

More than anyone else, the Japanese have faithfully accepted and implemented the subject of modern historical studies. Japanese scholars took modern historical studies—that is, world history—which only dealt with Western history, and by applying and forcibly expanding it to East Asia, that part of the world to which Japan is geographically adjacent, created the scholarly fields of Japanese and Eastern historical studies.

Furthermore, the field of Japanese historical studies was systematized without trouble. Eastern historical studies, by contrast, has encountered extreme difficulty in this regard. Its discrepancies remain unresolved to this day.

Systematization in this context refers to building an overall history by periodization, which represents "advancement" and "progress" at the stages of history (i.e., Western history) of "ancient times," "the Middle Ages," and "the modern era" that the West has traversed. This was standard practice in historical studies. It mattered little whether such studies pertained to Marxist history (a school of post–World War II Japanese historical studies) or some other Western system.

A classic text of such Japanese historical studies is *Chuseiteki sekai no keisei* (Formation of a Medieval World), written in 1944 by historian Ishimoda Sho (1912–1986). Set in Kuroda manor, Iga Province, which was operated by Todaiji Temple much as a fief, the book depicts how a "Middle Age" was born and undone in Japan, thereby dynamically presenting the historical changes that occurred in the prevailing society of the time.

Not only that, but the range covered by the book extended to the formation of a Middle Age in Japan as a whole, and the lack of such a period in China, making it wholly consistent with Marx's understanding. The book signified an achievement of Japanese historical studies, which had been captivated by Marxist history.

Marxist history has long since become passé as a foundational theory. However, in an appendix to Ishimoda's work, historian Ishii Susumu

(1931–2001) commented that in terms of contrast with China in particular, the perception of Japan as the only country in Asia that could have formed a Middle Age exhibited both consciously and unconsciously a disparity between Japanese history and Asian history, with Chinese history being one illustrative example of the latter. There is scope for further serious thought on this matter.

Then what historical course did early modern Japan follow? Let us take a broad look.

The Archipelago up to Early Modern Times

The Japanese archipelago is located at the eastern end of Eurasia, and across water at that. There is practically no land east of there. In other words, it is the farthest reach of the world, and backward to boot.

This is why Japan, since its beginnings as a country, has proactively adopted the advanced cultures and structures of mainland China and the Korean Peninsula, attempting to adapt to the Asian historical context. These processes constitute the ancient history of Japan, one aspect of which is represented by the concept of *ritsuryo kokka* (a nation based on a government of law).

In the post-Mongol era, however, the archipelago clearly moved in the opposite direction, distancing itself from Asia. An exemplar of this trend would be the classical Chinese writing system and written language imported to Japan from the continent and the peninsula.

Among the uses of Chinese writing in Japan, the first such difference was a written language based on Chinese translations of Buddhist texts. The Buddhist faith became indigenized in Japan through its constant syncretizing with the traditional Japanese faith of Shinto. Around this same period, the Chinese writing system was also indigenized, chiefly by the invention of the kana syllabaries; thus, the Japanese culture, belief, thought, and the mother tongue that provides the foundation for all of these became far removed from the original classical Chinese.

The formation of early modern Japan made the break irrevocable. Feudal lords who rose up from the lower ranks drove out such traditional elites as Buddhist priests and imperial court nobles, and monopolized the military and the government—a case of the low supplanting the high.

In the course of this process, these lords also carried out a thorough suppression of religious sects and doctrines and their devotees—such as Christianity or the Ikko Ikki uprising of farmers and local samurai who were adherents of Jodo Shinshu, a major Buddhist sect—that inclined toward political action and authority of one or another sort. We might say that they effected a kind of separation of politics and religion as a result.

The peaceful Edo period, with its proliferation of Confucianism, was no different in this regard. Confucianism spread among the people as well as the state, and through it many Japanese mastered classical Chinese, which raised the overall intellectual level of the country. The Edo *bakufu* (the Tokugawa shogunate) attempted to govern by influencing the population through scholarship and culture, particularly in Confucianism. It also prohibited studying subjects other than neo-Confucianism, which was its own governing ideology, as part of an effort to raise neo-Confucianism's profile among its people. Yet the doctrine of Confucianism never became the sort of structural or educational doctrine that would regulate government or society, as it did on the continent or the peninsula. Furthermore, civil society began to experience what might be termed an allergic reaction to Confucianism, and the more positivist studies of *rangaku* ("Western sciences through the Dutch language") as well as *kokugaku* ("national learning") increased in popularity. As an aside, the latter was an academic movement, a school of Japanese philology and philosophy that originated in the Tokugawa (i.e., Edo) period.

Even though the Japanese acquired proficiency in classical Chinese, they never mastered the Confucianist concepts or ideology that should have been indivisible from the language. In this regard, even as Japan used the same classical Chinese as the continent and the peninsula, it remained significantly removed from both, where Confucianism had instead achieved a degree of universality.

"Great Development": Advance and Standstill

Japan's Sengoku period of conflict among rival warlords overlapped with the Age of Discovery. The archipelago, with extensive lodes of gold and silver, reveled in a commercial boom with these precious metals as capital. The economy was invigorated, and society became affluent.

Accumulated wealth and energy drove a tremendous development effort in public works. A particularly important project was river improvement and irrigation engineering, which turned unreclaimed floodplains into fertile rice paddies.

In the three hundred years culminating in the eighteenth century, land under cultivation roughly tripled to some three million *chobu* (approx. 7.4 million acres), and new villages were being built in rapid succession. And lords great and small who governed these lands competed in the building of castle towns. The farming villages and cities of modern Japan were created in this era. Early modern Japan was truly a period of "great development," a reformation of the archipelago. It was also during this time that the population roughly tripled, from ten to thirty million.

By the start of the eighteenth century, however, this "great development" plateaued, and there were no further noticeable increases in either arable land or population. Quantitative limits had been reached.

Veins of precious metals were depleted, and there were no more influential products that could be exported overseas. Notwithstanding, Asian products that had flooded Japan in the Age of Discovery—whether silk, tea, cotton, sugar, or the like—had long since become essentials of daily life. It was no longer possible to halt demand or supply for these.

A Socioeconomic Conversion

Japanese society accordingly underwent a metamorphosis. Agriculture, which had revolved around production of primary grains such as rice and barley, converted to the production of local specialty products, taking advantage of the characteristics of the various regions. Simply put, this was a change to domestic production of Chinese products that Japan had thus far had to import. Production of silk, tea, cotton, and sugar began all over the country. Eventually, self-sustaining domestic supply of such goods became possible. The same was true of such products from the Americas as sweet potatoes and tobacco that also arrived during the same era.

From the outset, these specialty products were commercial goods. As they were each concentrated in specific manufacturing sites, shipping and allocation were necessary, giving rise to transport, conveyance, and commerce. A distribution market emerged, albeit one that was limited to domestic Japanese operations, constrained as it was by *sakoku*. The authorities proactively engaged in administration and regulation by such means as forming merchant guilds. A market economy in which the public and private sectors were integrated thus arose at this time.

Peasant labor sustained both this industrial transformation and market economy formation. Bringing about a qualitative switch in a confined, limited land area while preserving quantitative production levels could only be accomplished by concentrated investment of labor and funds. A feudal system arose in which the following became commonplace: land taxation, paid in kind by farmers, who worked continuously for a given lord, by giving their lord their produce; the thorough cyclical use of natural resources, in which, for example, townspeople sold or exchanged their excreta to the farmers as fertilizer, and then bought the produce that the farmers grew with that very fertilizer; and recycling, in such forms as pawnbrokers and secondhand clothing stores.

This activity could not be made more efficient solely by the private sector. There was a risk of disorderly overcutting of forests, and conflicts could also occur in areas where farmlands spanned multiple villages. Authority would have to be wielded to manage and coordinate these, even more so when large-scale public works projects were needed. As the authorities united with the private sector, the development, preservation, and utilization of nature proliferated.

Thus, the archipelago in the eighteenth century assembled an industrial structure independent of Asian trade, by becoming self-sufficient in silk, tea, cotton, and sugar. And this was true not only of Japan: it happened in Europe at the same time.

Europe accomplished this feat by transplanting products to colonies and mechanizing labor—that is, the Industrial Revolution. Japan, for its part, achieved similar self-sufficiency through domestic cultivation and the work of the peasantry: herein lie the distinctive features of Japan. Whereas Europe formed world markets and economies on global scales, Japan too created a market economy, albeit on a smaller scale and almost completely domestic.

In both cases, government and economy, authority and the private sector, had close relations. As with Europe, Japanese society had a structure that integrated high and low in a strongly cohesive manner.

Japanese History, Asian History, and Europe

As seen in the preceding section, various distinctive features of Asian history are almost entirely absent from Japanese history. If anything, Japan has followed a historical evidentiary process in which its similarities with, or parallels to, Europe stand out.

First, the dual zones of nomads and farmers that constituted the dynamics of Asian history were absent from the archipelago. Accordingly, Japan lacked military power with supreme mobility as well as commerce and finance that would connect remote regions. Alliances between these also inevitably did not emerge. Like medieval Europe, Japan was a unitary zone in which agricultural production took priority. In addition, there was little of the binary social structure in which government and economy, the authorities and the private sector, are prone to grow apart from one another. It was an unwritten rule in Edo-period Japan that "farmers should neither be killed nor allowed to live"; that is, the authorities kept a watchful eye over them—another strong similarity to Europe.

Japanese used Chinese characters—that is, classical Chinese—from the continent as their writing system. However, they did not adopt Confucianism or neo-Confucianism as a political or social ideology, as happened on the continent and the Korean Peninsula. This was true from the daily lives of Japanese people to domestic organization and foreign relations.

There is a theory that labels foreign relations in early modern Japan as "the Sinocentric system, Japanese-style," with the Tokugawa shogunate at the summit. This is, however, unlike the real Sinocentric system, in that it merely uses Confucianist vocabulary and concepts common in the Edo period to describe and express the separate relations that Japan had with Korea, the Ryukyu Islands, the Netherlands, and the Ainu.

The archipelago was also removed from Mongol traditions that were revered by the nomadic nations of the Asian inland. Though they shared the Buddhist faith, Japanese Buddhism, based on the Chinese translations of Buddhist texts, was syncretized with Shinto, and was practically unconnected with the Theravada Buddhism or Tibetan Buddhism commonly practiced across Asia.

Moreover, early modern Japan, from the time of warlords Oda Nobunaga and Toyotomi Hideyoshi to the early Edo period (from the end of the seventeenth to the beginning of the eighteenth century), effected a kind of separation of politics and religion by subordinating Buddhism and banning Christianity. Here too is another parallel with Europe at the same time, from the Protestant Reformation to the Thirty Years' War.

The same is true of economics. If the Industrial Revolution in eighteenth-century Europe amounted to the substitution of imports of Asian products with domestic production thereof, then Japan too accomplished a similar substitution of imports with domestic production in the eighteenth century, even if by different means. We may treat this as another parallel development.

After the Industrial Revolution, on the other hand, Europe formed world economies and markets, and having caught up with Asian economies, proceeded to surpass them by means of imperialism. This was total world domination.

By contrast, however parallel the development, the economy and markets of *sakoku* Japan were restricted to the archipelago. It was all Japan could do to keep up with the Asian economies. Europe dwarfed it, in speed and scale.

This is why, having understood the modern West and early modern Japan, and discerned the latter, Marx propounded the great insight that

Japan "gives a much truer picture of the European middle ages than all our history books." That being the case, Meiji-period Japan had to engage anew with Westernization and modernization.

Modern Japan and the Present-Day World

In this way, the Japanese archipelago's history lacks similarities with Asian history and East Asia, and in fact has much more in common with Europe and the West. Despite that historical commonality, the archipelago is geographically adjacent to East Asia and has undeniable linguistic and cultural aspects in common with the region, as exemplified by the Chinese language. These characteristics of Japan provided vital conditions in terms of driving the transformation and reorganization of East Asia beginning in the twentieth century.

The *bunmei kaika* (civilization and enlightenment) of Meiji Japan exhaustively copied the "modern era" onto the base of a socioeconomic structure approximating Marx's "picture of the European middle ages." That the country was more or less able to achieve "promotion of industry" in economics and "enhancing the wealth and military might of the country" in politics was due to the creation of that social structure having followed a historical process close to that of the West.

Bunmei kaika was an attempt by the Japanese to acquire perfect command of Western "modern" sovereign state structures and military and economic systems. To that end, it was incumbent upon the Japanese people to comprehend, consider, and express "modernity" in their own language. It would have been difficult to translate Western technical vocabulary and concepts using *Yamato-kotoba*, the purely native Japanese language, as the latter was a relatively recent development, historically speaking. Thus, they employed the Chinese language instead. The trajectory of Japan's modern history was that of achieving Westernization by means of Chinese—that is, loanwords from Chinese that had long since effectively become the Japanese vernacular.

And in imitating the West up to and including imperialism, Japan tried to subjugate the neighboring region of East Asia. In the midst of this effort,

Japan foisted its own brand of modernization on the Korean Peninsula and mainland China. That the peninsula and the continent effectively emulated this while strongly resisting it is itself due to their having the Chinese language in common. As a result, the old East Asian order underwent a metamorphosis beginning at the linguistic and conceptual levels.

Nor was this true only of East Asia. To varying degrees, Japan's pioneering practice of modernization had an impact on the rest of Asia, inspiring movements that aimed to use Westernization to reject subjugation by the Western powers.

Of course, the Japanese could not have planned all of this themselves. Even so, they played no small part. That all manner of countries in the present-day world constitute for the time being an international society on Western standards is due to the building of a consensus that Westernization is the correct choice. We can say that the existence of Japan is outstanding in this sense.

But Japan's historical experience is by no means the same as East or West Asian history. With regard to so-called international society—that is, Western standards—diversity in attitudes, speech, and conduct is inevitable among Japan; East Asia, in proximity to Japan; and West Asia, distant from Japan. Much of the East Asian state of affairs, which is harsh when it comes to such questions as historical awareness and territorial dominion, arises from said diversity, in much the same manner as the many terrorist incidents and other conflicts in West Asia.

However, the vast majority of Japanese do not realize this, because they cannot free themselves from the preconception of being ill-informed about the truths of Asian history, promptly treating Western history as world history, and casually conflating Japan with East Asia. The prevalence of "global history" exemplifies this condition. A world history with Asian history as its cornerstone is essential.

There is more to the world than just Japan and the West. There is a need to contemplate everyday realities anew and reconsider world history. This must be our intent, as we face an era, a world, overflowing with risk.

AFTERWORD

Passages from things we read in our youth frequently linger in memory. For this author, it is this apt remark from "Sekaishi josetsu" (A Primer on World History) by Miyazaki Ichisada, included in *Ajia shiron* (Essays on Asian History):

> From beginning to end, history is the history of a single world. It is not a question of whether world history is possible. History the way it ought to be can take no shape other than that of world history.

Miyazaki was the sage and maestro of Eastern historical studies, and these words could only have come from one of such status. That said, the first time I read this text, I simply thought, "True enough." I was in no position to fully appreciate the grounds or circumstances that led him to make this statement. I happened to hit upon it only after I turned fifty.

There are two implications here: that Eastern historical studies are essential, and yet unnecessary, to world history "the way it ought to be."

The study of history was founded in Europe; there was no such thing in Asia. There is thus a degree of inevitability in that the professed "world history" of humankind initially became Western history, for all intents and purposes. One cannot think of something when that thing does not exist.

The Japanese invented Eastern historical studies in order to correct this bias. This was necessary so long as the tendency to treat only Western history as "world history" persisted. Conceiving of a history of all of humankind and narrating a true world history require standing on the accomplishments of Eastern historical studies and constantly checking the subjectivity and prejudice of Western history and modern intellect fancying themselves to be "world history."

Once we have attained this state, however, Eastern history will have become superfluous, a white elephant. Accordingly, the ultimate aim of Eastern historical studies is to one day render its existence unnecessary and for it to be sublimated into world history "the way it ought to be."

When I look around, I find vast quantities of books that profess to be "world history." Regrettably, the fact is that their positions are at odds; they have neither the hopes, the accomplishments, the sensibility, nor the mission of Eastern historical studies.

That being so, the raison d'être of Eastern history must be retained, even as it is a means, a method, for achieving a genuine world history. Whereas there may be leeway to consider extenuating circumstances regarding the ignorance of Westerners and Western history about the meaning of Eastern historical studies, it is annoying that specialists in Eastern and Asian history—to say nothing of Japanese history—are similarly uninformed on this point.

It is not only the words of Miyazaki Ichisada that must be remembered. Another text, *What Is History?*, written by British political scientist and historian Edward Hallett Carr (1892–1982), advocates that "history is 'a selective system,'" and that historical narrative arises from the process of selection.

While these may be more or less axiomatic to students of history, it is unusual for these theses to be treated so lightly. History books labeled world or complete histories, whether textbooks or academic works, are invariably collaborative efforts if they go beyond advocacy and conceptualization. While this may be a "system" and "selective," it does not follow that this is a "selective system."

In this present period of information science and globalization, all manner of minute historical evidence has come to our attention. No one person can hope to find or learn such innumerable quantities of historical fact. A certain amount of specialization and cooperation is thus unavoidable, and also useful, when it comes to scrutiny of these facts. That alone, however, will not produce a rational complete world history. There needs to be a selection of historical evidence. As it will not do to pick and choose at random, a consistent system is essential. And Japanese historians have a propensity to rely on Western theories in this regard. While it might be fair to do so if these theories were right, it seems to be the story of Japanese historical studies to perpetually get these theories wrong.

Whether traditional world history (i.e., Western history) or the latest global history, the reason for not choosing these selective systems is that they are useless when it comes to selecting the historical facts that matter to Asia past and present. We can affirm that those who have personally dealt with Asian history should properly understand, and those who do not feel this way are not truly confronting Asian historical sources. The need thereby arises to survey the world with the eyes of one who knows the systems of Eastern historical studies, and to compose a complete history by one's own hand.

The viewpoint is East not West; the theory is not the newest on the scene but one restored, revivified. Academic fact and truth are irrelevant to the trends and currents of the times. This book is a world history narrative attempted from just such a standpoint, presuming throughout that it should be unnecessary. Although it is only an insignificant exercise in trial and error, its aim is presumptuously the same as that of the maestro Miyazaki, and in an excess of bravura, I dared to use the same title as that of Miyazaki's work for this one in the original Japanese.

This book is a compilation of sixteen installments of a column called "A Panoramic View of World History," originally serialized beginning December 2016 in *Chikuma*, a PR publication of Chikumashobo, publisher of the original Japanese edition. I have revised it to an extent, mainly cutting redundant descriptions. I received no small amount of assistance during the run of this column, which lasted more than a year. I wish to express my heartfelt gratitude to the following people in particular:

To Professor Kimizuka Naotaka, for unstinting encouragement and much gracious instruction about the history of England and Europe;

and Professor Yamashita Norihisa, for ever-perceptive critiques from a different specialty and point of view. Both of you kindly gave this dull, vacillating author the shove he needed.

And to Nagata Shiro, who guided this book from planning the original serialization to publication. Guided by your enthusiasm for working together to create a world history the way it ought to be, and by your magnanimity in tolerating my extremely bold and egoistic writing, I found it possible to exhibit an unfashionable recklessness to my heart's content.

Finally, to you, the learned reader, nothing would please me more than for you to accompany me in just such a world history.

Okamoto Takashi

May 2018

From the banks of the Kamo River, covered in new greenery

PRINCIPAL REFERENCES

In writing this book, I referred to a considerable number of texts, irrespective of whether I personally agreed with any given text or included it in the finished work. What follows is a select list of references, with care given to works that are readable and in accessible formats. I fervently hope that readers will peruse publications listed here in addition to those cited in the body of this book.

This list is by no means comprehensive. For reasons of space, well-known classic texts such as those by Hegel, Lenin, Marx, or Wallerstein have been omitted, except where directly quoted. I have also refrained from enumerating voluminous academic texts to the extent practicable and have only included foreign language works available in Japanese translation.

These constraints are necessary to keep this list to a manageable length. I even left out Russian historian Vasily Vladimirovich Bartold, who by rights should come before anyone else. My having acted out of necessity according to "systems of selection" is hereby submitted for your consideration.

Titles are grouped by source language, Japanese followed by other languages, and in alphabetical order within each language category.

Japanese Publications

Fujisawa Michio. *Monogatari Itaria no rekishi: Kaitai kara toitsu made* [History of Italy: From Dissolution to Unification]. Tokyo: Chuokoronsha, 1991.

Hamashita Takeshi and Kawakatsu Heita, eds. *Ajia koekiken to Nihon kogyoka 1500–1900* [Intra-Asian Trade Area and Industrialization in Japan 1500–1900]. Tokyo: Libroport, 1991.

Hara Yonosuke. *Ajia-gata keizai shisutemu: Gurobarizumu ni koshite* [An Asia-Style Economic System: Defying Globalism]. Tokyo: Chuokoron Shinsha, 2000.

Hasegawa Takahiko. *Sangyo kakumei* [The Industrial Revolution]. Tokyo: Yamakawa Shuppansha, 2012.

Hayashi Kayoko. *Osuman teikoku no jidai* [The Ottoman Empire Period]. Tokyo: Yamakawa Shuppansha, 1997.

Honda Minobu. *Mongoru jidaishi kenkyu* [Historical Studies on the Mongol Domination]. Tokyo: University of Tokyo Press, 1991.

Iizuka Koji. *Toyo shi to Seiyo shi to no aida* [Between Eastern and Western History]. Tokyo: Iwanami Shoten, 1963.

Ishida Mikinosuke. *Zotei Choan no haru* [Springtime in Chang'an, rev. ed.]. Commentary by Enoki Kazuo. Tokyo: Heibonsha, 1967.

Ishimoda Sho. *Chuseiteki sekai no keisei* [Formation of a Medieval World]. Tokyo: Iwanami Shoten, 1985.

Kawakatsu Heita. *Nihon bunmei to kindai Seiyo: "Sakoku" saiko* [Japanese Civilization and the Modern West: Rethinking Japanese Seclusion]. Tokyo: NHK Publishing, 1991.

———. *Bunmei no kaiyo shikan* [A Maritime Historical View of Civilization]. Tokyo: Chuokoronsha, 1997.

Kawakita Minoru. *Sato no sekaishi* [A World History of Sugar]. Tokyo: Iwanami Shoten, 1996.

———. "Purotesutantizumu dakara hatten? Sangyo kakumei ga okita honto no riyu" [Advancement Due to Protestantism? The Real Reason for the Industrial Revolution]. *Weekly Toyo Keizai*, no. 6677 (Aug. 13–20), 2016.

Kimizuka Naotaka. *Monogatari Igirisu no rekishi (Jo): Kodai Buriten-to kara Erizabesu issei made* [History of Great Britain (Part 1): From Ancient Britain to the Age of Queen Elizabeth I]. Tokyo: Chuokoron Shinsha, 2015.

Kimura Shozaburo. *Rekishi no hakken: Atarashii sekaishizo no teisho* [Discovering History: Proposal for a New Image of World History]. Tokyo: Chuokoronsha, 1968.

Kishimoto Mio. *Higashi Ajia no "kinsei"* ["The Early Modern Era" in East Asia]. Tokyo: Yamakawa Shuppansha, 1998.

Kosugi Yasushi. *Isuramu to wa nani ka: Sono shukyo, shakai, bunka* [What Is Islam? Religion, Society, Culture]. Tokyo: Kodansha, 1994.

Kuroda Akinobu. *Kahei shisutemu no sekaishi: "Hitaishosei" o yomu* [A World History of the Currency System: Reading "Asymmetry"]. Tokyo: Iwanami Shoten, 2003.

Kuwabara Jitsuzo. *Ho Juko no jiseki*. Tokyo: Heibonsha, 1989. Translated as "On P'u Shou-keng," *Memoirs of the Research Department of the Toyo Bunko*, no. 2 (1928): 1–79, and no. 7 (1935): 1–104.

Mano Eiji. *Shinsho Toyo shi [8] Chuo Ajia no rekishi: Sogen to oashisu no sekai* [New Eastern History 8: History of Central Asia: Steppe and Oasis Worlds]. Tokyo: Kodansha, 1977.

Masuda Shiro. *Yoroppa to wa nani ka* [What Is Europe?]. Tokyo: Iwanami Shoten, 1967.

Matsuda Hisao. *Ajia no rekishi: Tozai kosho kara mita zenkindai no sekaizo* [History of Asia: An Image of the Pre-Modern World Seen from East-West Interactions]. Tokyo: Iwanami Shoten, 1992.

Matsui Toru. *Sekai shijo no keisei* [Formation of a World Market]. Tokyo: Iwanami Shoten, 1991.

Miyazaki Ichisada. *Ajia shiron* [Essays on Asian History]. Tokyo: Chuokoron Shinsha, 2002.

——. *Chugoku shi* [History of China]. Tokyo: Iwanami Shoten, 2015.

——. *Tozai kosho shiron* [Essays on the History of East-West Interaction]. Edited by Tonami Mamoru. Tokyo: Chuokoronsha, 1998.

Mizumoto Kunihiko. *Zenshu Nihon no rekishi daijukkan: Tokugawa no kokka dezain* [Collected Works of Japanese History, vol. 10: The Design of the Tokugawa State]. Tokyo: Shogakukan, 2008.

Morimoto Kazuo, ed. *Perushia-go ga musunda sekai: Mo hitotsu no Yurashia shi* [The World Connected by the Persian Language: Another Eurasian History]. Sapporo: Hokkaido University Press, 2009.

Moriyasu Takao. *Shiruku Rodo to To teikoku: Kobo no sekaishi 05* [The Silk Road and The Tang Empire: What Is Human History? vol. 5]. Tokyo: Kodansha, 2007.

Okada Hidehiro. *Sekaishi no tanjo: Mongoru no hatten to dento* [The Birth of World History: Mongol Advancement and Tradition]. Tokyo: Chikumashobo, 1999.

Okamoto Takashi. *Chugoku "han-Nichi" no genryu* [Origins of "Anti-Japaneseness" in China]. Tokyo: Kodansha, 2011.

——. *Kindai Chugoku shi* [Modern Chinese History]. Tokyo: Chikumashobo, 2013.

Okazaki Katsuyo. *Seisho vs. sekaishi: Kirisutokyoteki rekishikan to wa nani ka* [The Bible vs. World History: What Is a Christian Historical Perspective?]. Tokyo: Kodansha, 1996.

Sakurai Kunitomo. *Taiyo kokuten ga kataru bunmeishi: "Shohyogaki" to kindai no seiritsu* [A History of Civilization as Told by Sunspots: The "Little Ice Age" and the Founding of the Modern Era]. Tokyo: Chuokoronsha, 1987.

Sugiyama Masaaki. *Mongoru teikoku no kobo (Jo) (Ge)* [Rise and Fall of the Mongol Empire (Volumes 1 and 2)]. Tokyo: Kodansha, 1996.

——. *Yubokumin kara mita sekaishi: Minzoku mo kokkyo mo koete* [World History from a Nomadic Viewpoint: Transcending Nations and Borders]. Tokyo: Nikkei Business Publications, 1997.

Takayama Hiroshi. *Chusei Shichiria okoku* [The Norman Kingdom of Sicily]. Tokyo: Kodansha, 1999.

Tamaki Toshiaki. *Kindai Yoroppa no tanjo: Oranda kara Igirisu e* [The Birth of Modern Europe: From the Netherlands to England]. Tokyo: Kodansha, 2009.

Umesao Tadao. *Bunmei no seitai shikan*. Tokyo: Chuokoronsha, 1974. Translated by Beth Carey as *An Ecological View of History: Japanese Civilization in the World Context* (Tokyo: Trans Pacific Press, 2003).

English, French, and German Publications

Bagehot, Walter. *The English Constitution*. London: Chapman and Hall, 1867. Translated by Komatsu Haruo as *Igirisu kenseiron* (Tokyo: Chuokoron Shinsha, 2011).

Barnes, Julian. *A History of the World in 10 1/2 Chapters*. London: Jonathan Cape, 1989. Translated by Tanji Ai and Tanji Toshie as *10 1/2 sho de kakareta sekai no rekishi* (Tokyo: Hakusuisha, 1991).

Brewer, John. *The Sinews of Power: War, Money, and the English State, 1688–1783*. New York: Alfred A. Knopf, 1989. Translated by Okubo Keiko as *Zaisei-Gunji kokka no shogeki: Senso, kane, Igirisu kokka 1688–1783* (Nagoya: University of Nagoya Press, 2003).

Carr, Edward Hallett. *What Is History?* London: Macmillan, 1961. Translated by Shimizu Ikutaro as *Rekishi to wa nani ka* (Tokyo: Iwanami Shoten, 1962).

Crossley, Pamela Kyle. *What Is Global History?* Cambridge, UK: Polity Press, 2008. Translated by Sato Shoichi as *Gurobaru hisutori to wa nani ka* (Tokyo: Iwanami Shoten, 2012).

Frank, Andre Gunder. *ReOrient: Global Economy in the Asian Age*. Berkeley: University of California Press, 1998. Translated by Yamashita Norihisa as *Ri-Oriento: Ajia jidai no gurobaru ekonomi* (Tokyo: Fujiwara Shoten, 2000).

Hicks, Sir John Richard. *A Theory of Economic History*. Oxford: Oxford University Press, 1969. Translated by Shinbo Hiroshi and Watanabe Fumio as *Keizaishi no riron* (Tokyo: Kodansha, 1995).

Jones, Eric Lionel. *The European Miracle: Environments, Economies and Geopolitics in the History of Europe and Asia*. Cambridge, UK: Cambridge University Press, 1981. Translated by Yasumoto Minoru and Wakimura Kohei as *Yoroppa no kiseki: Kankyo, keizai, chisei no hikakushi* (Nagoya: University of Nagoya Press, 2000).

Lippmann Abu-Lughod, Janet. *Before European Hegemony: The World System A.D. 1250–1350*. New York: Oxford University Press, 1989. Translated in two volumes by Sato Tsugitaka, Shiba Yoshinobu, Takayama Hiroshi, and Miura Toru as *Yoroppa haken izen (Jo) (Ge)* (Tokyo: Iwanami Shoten, 2001).

Maddison, Angus. *The World Economy: A Millennial Perspective*. Paris: OECD Development Centre, 2001. Translated by the Institute of Politics and Economy, supervised by Kanamori Hisao, as *Kezai tokei de miru sekai keizai 2000nen-shi* (Tokyo: Kashiwa Shobo, 2004).

Mahbubani, Kishore. *The Great Convergence: Asia, the West, and the Logic of One World*. New York: Public Affairs, 2013. Translated by Yamamoto Fumihito as *Daishuren: Bocho-suru chusan kaikyu ga sekai o kaeru* (Tokyo: Chuokoron Shinsha, 2015).

Marx, Karl. *Capital: A Critique of Political Economy*. Vol. 1. Translated into English by Samuel Moore and Edward Aveling, edited by Frederick Engels. Revised and amplified by Ernest Untermann. Chicago: Charles H. Kerr & Company, 1909.

https://www.marxists.org/archive/marx/works/download/pdf/Capital-Volume-I. pdf. Translated into Japanese in four parts by Shihonron Honyaku Iinkai as *Shihonron* (Tokyo: Shin-Nihon Shuppansha, 1982–1983).

Meinecke, Friedrich. *Die Entstehung des Historismus*. Munich: R. Oldenbourg Verlag, 1936. Translated by Kikumori Hideo and Aso Ken as *Rekishishugi no seiritsu* (Tokyo: Chikumashobo, 1968).

Pearson, Michael Naylor. *Merchants and Rulers in Gujarat: The Response to the Portuguese in the Sixteenth Century*. Berkeley, CA: University of California Press, 1976. Translated by Ikuta Shigeru as *Porutogaru to Indo: Chusei Gujarato no shonin to shihaisha* (Tokyo: Iwanami Shoten, 1984).

Pomeranz, Kenneth L. *The Great Divergence: China, Europe, and the Making of the Modern World Economy*. Princeton, NJ: Princeton University Press, 2001. Translated and supervised by Kawakita Minoru as *Daibunki: Chugoku, Yoroppa, soshite kindai sekai keizai no keisei* (Nagoya: University of Nagoya Press, 2015).

Schumpeter, Joseph Alois. *History of Economic Analysis*. London: Routledge, 1987. Translated in three volumes by Tobata Seiichi and Fukuoka Masao as *Keizai bunseki no rekishi* (Tokyo: Iwanami Shoten, 2005–2006).

Torr, Dona, ed. *Marx on China: 1853–1860*. London: Lawrence & Wishart, 1951. Translated by Takayama Rintaro as *Marukusu Chugoku ron* (Tokyo: Toko Shoin, 1973).

Vidal de la Blache, Paul. *Principles of Human Geography*. Translated from the French by Millicent Todd Bingham. New York: Henry Holt and Company, 1926. Translated in two volumes by Iizuka Koji as *Jinbun chirigaku genri* (Tokyo: Iwanami Shoten, 1940).

INDEX

Notes: Page numbers in *italic* refer to illustrations. The letter "t" after a page number refers to tables. The letter "f" after a page number refers to figures. Subentries indicate related themes in the main body of the text.

China, 151, 152, 152f; ancient civilizations, 51–52, 58, 61, 62, 63; Asian history and, 16–17, 17f, 18, 19, 23, 24, 27, 31, 33, 34, 36, 37f; classical texts/archives, 9, 10, 62, 80, 81; commerce and mercantile trade, 151, 152, 169, 170, 182, 184; homogenization of "Chinese-ness," 142, 143, 143f, 144, 145, 146, 147f; Middle Ages and, 196–98, 199; migration era (Asia), 53, 74, 77, 78, 94, 95, 96, 97; modern West, 170, 182, 184, 188, 191, 196–97, 198, 199, 205, 206; Mongol Empire and post-Mongol empires, 109, 113, 115, 116, 124, 128, 130, 131, 132, 148; periodization structures, 30

Choan no haru (Springtime in Chang'an) (Ishida), 77

Christianity, 13–15, 16; ancient civilizations, 57, 58, 59, 59, 60; migration era (Asia), 66, 71, 72, 73; modern West, 157, 158, 160–62, 165, 166, 170, 193, 194, 200, 204; Mongol Empire and post-Mongol empires, 137, 138, 140

Church of Rome. *See* Roman Catholic Church

city-states (polis), 30, 31, 47, 163, 165, 168, 169, 175

classical Chinese (language), 62, 147, 147f, 199, 200, 203, 205

climatic variations, 105, 131, 132, 143, 158, 160, 171; ancient civilizations, 53–54, 55, 56, 57, 74, 77; Turks and Turkic khaganate, 93–94, 95, 97

coal industry, 97, 171, 189

colonialism, 145, 168, 173, 185f, 187, 203

Columbus, Christopher, 13, 148, 166, 167, 168

commerce and mercantile trade, 197, 201–3; ancient civilizations, 33–35, 39f,

40, 41, 46–47, 55; maritime trade, 36, 145, 148–49, 168, 169–72, 173f, 174–76; migration era (Asia), 90, 91, 92–93; Ming dynasty, 144–45; modern West, 156, 160, 164, 174, 181, 185, 185f, 190, 191, 193; Mongol Empire, 120, 121–22, 125–27, 128, 128, 129, 130, 133, 134

communications, 39f, 40, 41, 47, 108

compagnie (corporate organizations) (Western Europe), 164–65

Confucianism, 58, 61, 62, 81; Age of Discovery, 142, 143, 147f, 148; Japan and, 200, 203, 204

conquest dynasties, 147

Constantine the Great, 59, 59

Constantinople (Nova Roma/Istanbul), 59, 67f, 71, 73, 87f, 118f, 137–38, 140, 159f, 163

Cordoba, 54f, 87f, 158, 159f

cotton industry, 144, 145, 151, 201, 202; maritime empires, 169, 173, 173f, 182, 183–84, 183f, 185f

credit systems, 164, 180, 184, 185–87, 191

Crimea, 136f, 138–39

"Crisis of the Fourteenth Century," 131–32, 141, 144, 166

Crusades, The, 89, 92, 131, 138, 160, 161, 163, 171

Ctesiphon, 67f, 68, 70, 70f

currency systems, 127, 128, 128, 129, 142, 144, 163, 164, 165, 167, 180

D

Dadu (Cambaluc), 124, 129, 132, 142

Da Gama, Vasco, 148, 167

Dai-ön Yeke Mongol Uls (Yuan dynasty): achievements of the Mongol Empire, *116*, 117, 118f, 119, 124, 125; post-Mongol empires, 130, 132, 141, 142, 146–47, 148, 149

Damascus, 71, 84, 114, 118f

Dark Ages. *See* Middle Ages

Das Kapital (Marx), 16, 194, 195, 196–97, 198, 204, 205

denko/dianhu ("peasant," "tenant farmer," "serf") (Japan/China), 31

disease, 24, 54, 131, 166

E

early modern Asia: achievements of the Mongol Empire, 117–18, 118f, 119–23, 123f, 124–28, *128*, 129; Age of Discovery, 19, 134, 148–49, 150, 152, 200; building the Mongol Empire, 104–5, *105*, 106–8, 106f, *108*, 109–11, 110f, 111f, 112–13, 112f, 114–16, *116*; modern West, 178, 179, 191–92, 193; Ming-Qing transition, 132, 141–43, 143f, 144–47, 147f, 148–49; post-Mongol empires, 129–34, 134f, 135–36, 136f, 137–40

East Asia, 10, 15, 197, 198, 205, 206; Buddhism, 60–63, 61f, *62*; history of East-West interactions, 33, 34, 35, 35f, 36–37, 38, 43; homogeneity with the West, 18–20, 21, 22, 26; Migration period (Europe), 55, 57, 58; migration era (Asia), 74, 75, 77, 78–79, 83; modern West, 166, 171, 176, 189, 190; Mongol Empire and post-Mongol empires, 105, 106, 109, 116, 121, 137, 140–42, 143, 146, 147, 148; Turks and Turkic khaganate, 89, 90, 91, 94, 95, 97, 98, 99f, 100

Eastern historical studies (*Toyo shi*), 96, 130, 198, 207, 208, 209; East-West differential, 23–24; present state of, 30–31, 32, 33, 35; Japanese conception of world history, 9, 10, 11, 20–23, 25, 26

Eastern Orthodox Church, 138, 140

Eastern Roman (Byzantine) Empire, 138, 158, 159f, 163, 165; ancient civilizations, 54f, 56, 60; migration era (Asia), 66, *66*, 67, 67f, 68, 69, 70–71, 70f, 73, 83f, 87f. *See also* Rome and Roman Empire

Eastern and Western Steppes, 105–6, 106f, 107, 108, 120, 124

East Eurasia, 78–79, 80, 81, 82–83

East-West interactions, 33, 34, 35, 35f, 36–37, 38, 43

ecological historical approach, 17, 24, 45; regional demarcation, 35, 35f, 36, 37, 38, 39f, 42f, 43

economic history, 17, 17f, 18, 23, 174, 204

Ecumenical Patriarchate of Constantinople, 138

Edo period (Japan), 33, 170, 197, 200, 203, 204

Egypt, 68, 70, 84, 85, 86, 114, 117; ancient civilizations, 47, 48, 48f, 50, 56

energy resources, 45, 97, 171, 183, 184, 187, 189, 201

England, 135, 164, 167, 170; advent of, 173, 173f, 174, 175, 176, 177, 177f, *177*, 178, *178*, 179; imperialism, 180, 181, 189, 196

English (language), 24, 126

Enlightenment, The, 16

equal-field system (J. *kindensei*), 57, 81–82

Eurasia, 90, 93; ancient civilizations, 34, 35, 38, 39, 39f, 40, 53; East Eurasia, 78–79, 80, 81, 82–83; Mongol Empire,

Iraq, 114

Ishida Mikinosuke, 77

Ishii Susumu, 198–99

Islam and Islamic World, 10; ancient civilizations, 58–59; emergence and triumph of, 66, 67, 68, 69, 69f, 70, 70f, 71, 72, 73, 74, 77, 79; migration era (Asia), 91–92, 92t, 93, 94; modern West, 158, 159, 160, 161, 166, 168, 171; Mongol Empire, 113–14, 118, 121; multipolarity of, 81, 83, 84–85, 86, 87, 87f, 88–89; post-Mongol empires, 133, 135, 136, 137–38, 139, 140, 141, 147, 147f, 149

Ismail I (Iran), 135

Ismailites, 113–14

Italy, 156–58, 159, 160, 161, 162–67, 168, 169, 171, 172, 175. *See also* Rome and Roman Empire (Western Roman Empire)

Iwami Ginzan Silver Mine (Japan), 152

J

jamchi (network of postal relay stations), 108, 109, 123f, 125

Japan, 119, 130–31, 145, 146, 148, 149, 152, 207, 209; "Great Development," 201; historical studies/Japanese history, 196, 197, 198–99; Middle Ages and, 196–98; modern West, 169–70, 173, 174, 179, 187; national character and history, 9, 14, 17f, 18, 19, 20–21; parallels with Europe, 203–5; pioneering historical conceptions, 35, 36–37, 37f, 38, 39, 39f; present-day world and, 205–6; religions/faith, 61, 62–63, 78–79, 80; socioeconomic conversion, 201–3; study of history of the West/East, 9–10, 11, 22, 23, 25–27, 30, 31, 32, 33; up to early modern times, 199–200, 201, 202

Jiangnan (China, south of Huai River), 63, 98, 100, 113, 115, 171; Mongol Empire and post-Mongol empires, 124, 129, 132, 141, 142, 143, 144, 150

Jin dynasty, 98, 99f, 100, 105, 106f, 109, 110f, 112f, 128

Jochi (son of Genghis Khan), 109, 111f; Uls, 118, 118f, 123f, 134f

Jodo Shinshu (Buddhist sect), 200

John, King of England (John Lackland), 178, *178*

joint-stock company, 186

Judaism, 58, 138

Judea, 59

Justinian, Emperor, 66, *66*, 67, 158

K

Kaiping, 112f, 116, 118f, 123f, 124

kana syllabic writing systems, 42f, 62–63, 199

kango (Sino-Japanese terminology), 33

Karakhanids, 87, 87f, 88, 89, 90, 91–92, 92t, 99f, 100

Karakorum, 108–9, 110f, 123f

Karluks, 83f, 87, 91, 99f

Kawakita Minoru, 19, 173f, 174

Khadijah (wife of Muhammad), 69, 69f

khalifa (caliphs), 69, 70f, 71, 86, 89, 114, 136

Khitai, 42f; achievements of the Mongol Empire, 120, 122, 124; building the Mongol Empire, 106, 108; Turks and Turkic khaganate, 94–96, 97, 98, 99f, 100–101

Khosrow I, King (Sasanian dynasty), *66*, 67, 68

Khosrow II, King (Sasanian dynasty), 68

Khubilai (grandson of Genghis Khan), 104, 111f, 112, 115, 116, *116*; achievements of the Mongol Empire, 117, 119, 123, 124, 125, 126, 127, 128; post-Mongol empires, 129, 130, 141, 142, 146, 149

Khwarezm-Shah dynasty, 106, 106f, 107, 120, 122, 136

Kipchaks, 106f, 110, 110f, 112, 118

kokugaku ("national learning") (Japan), 200

kokushi (national [Japanese] historical studies), 9

Korean Peninsula, 33, 36, 61, 78, 80, 199, 200, 203, 204, 206

Kumarajiva, 62

Kuwabara Jitsuzo, 130

L

language systems, 11, 22–23, 62, 88, 133, 147f, 199, 200, 203, 205, 206

"Last Judgment," 15

Lenin, Vladimir, 187

Li Shimin, Taizong (Emperor) of the Tang, 76, *76*

localism, 26–27

Lydia, 48, 48f

M

Machiavelli, Niccolò, 164

Maghreb, 84

Magna Carta, 178

Magyars, 55

Mahayana Buddhism, 61, 62, 63

Mamluk dynasty, 88, 94, 112f, 117, 118, 118f, 123f, 134f

Manchus, 146, 147f

Manichaeism, 58, 67, 73, 77, 91

maritime empires, 120, 167–73, 173f, 174–77, 177f, 178, 179–81

maritime trade, 36, 160, 165; Age of Discovery, 143, 145, 148–49, 150, 151, 152; post-Mongol empires, 123f, 129–31, 134

Marx, Karl, 16, 194, 195, 196–97, 198, 204, 205

matsurigoto (*matsuri*, administration of government), 57

Mauryan Empire, 50, 60

Ma Wara al-Nahr (Transoxania), 86, 88, 92, 107, 122, 166

Mazdakism, 67

Mecca, 68, 69, 70f, 87f, 106f, 110f, 112f, 118f, 123f, 134f, 136f, 138

Media, 48, 48f

medieval period (Europe). *See* Middle Ages

Medina (Yathrib, Madinat-al-Nabi/City of the Prophet), 69, 70f, 87f, 106f, 110f, 112f, 118f, 123f, 134f, 138

Mediterranean, The, 49, 56, 66, 71, 81, 83, 84, 85, 86; Italy and Sicily, 156–57, 158, 159, 159f, 161, 162, 163, 165, 166, 167; maritime empires, 168, 169, 170, 171, 172, 174; Mongol Empire and post-Mongol empires, 114, 131, 138, 149, 151, 152, 153

112, 118, 119–21, 123, 124–25, 126, 127; post-Mongol empires, 135, 137, 139–40, 141, 142, 143, 145, 146; Turks and Turkic khaganate, 90, 91, 92, 92t, 93, 94, 95–96, 97, 100, 101

Normans and Norman Conquest (Western Europe), 55, 159f, 160, 163, 176

numerical indices, 24

O

oasis cities and regions, 40, 41, 47, 51, 73, 90, 93, 96, 101, 165; Mongol Empire, 107, 108, 109, 111, 120, 126, 133

Oda Nobunaga, 204

Ögödei (son of Genghis Khan), 108, *108*, 109–10, 110f, 111, 111f, 119, 120, 162

Opium Wars, 184, 196

Orthodox Eastern Roman Christianity, 60

ortogh (business partnership/business), 126, 165

Ottoman Empire, 134f, 136, 136f, 137–39, 140, 141, 147, 153, 185f, 187, 192

P

Palermo, 158, 159f, 160, 161

Palestine, 163

Pamirs, 10, 38, 39f, 61f, 141; Mongol Empire, 122, 125, 126; Turks and Turkic khaganate, 88, 90, 91, 93

parliamentary system, 178, 179

Parthian dynasty, 50, 56

peasants and peasant labor, 31, 57, 81, 178, 202, 203

"perfect caliphs," 69f, 70–71, 70f

periodization structures, 21–23, 24, 30, 31, 32–33, 34, 35, 35f, 198

Persia: ancient civilizations, 47, 48, 49, 50, 51, 56, 58, 60, *66*; migration era (Asia), 67, 71, 84, 85–86, 88; Mongol Empire and post-Mongol empires, 121, 126, 133, 136, 151, 153

Persian (language), 85, 88, 92f, 100, 126, 133, 136

Phoenicia, 49, 71

Pisa (Italy), 159f, 160

pluralism and pluralistic coexistence, 25, 48, 49, 82, 162; early modern Asia, 130, 141, 142, 146, 147, 148

Poland, 110, 159f

Polytheism, 69

Pomeranz, Kenneth L., 18, 19, 25, 32, 189, 191

port cities, 160, 163

Portugal, 150, 168–69, 169–70, 170–71, 172, 173f, 174, 175, 181, 185f

Price Revolution, 167, 174

Protestantism, 59, 60, 204

public finance and banking, 129, 179–81, 184, 185–87, 190, 191, 193, 197

Pu Shougeng, 130

Q

Qara Khitai, 99f, 100, 101, 106, 107, 108, 120

Qin dynasty, 52, 74

Qing (Daicing Gurun [Great Qing]), 17f, 146–47, 147f, 148, 152, 153, 185f, 187, 192

Qin Shi Huang (first emperor of China), 52

Qocho (Uyghur kingdom), 87, 90, 91, 92, 92t, 99f, 100, 120, 122

quantitative economics, 23–24

R

rangaku ("Western sciences through the Dutch language") (Japan), 200

regional demarcation, 35, 35f, 37, 38–9, 39f, 42, 42f, 43

Renaissance, Italian, 157, 161, 162–65, 166, 179, 193, 194, 195

ritsuryo kokka (nation based on government of law), 199

ritsuryosei (political system) (Japan), 79, 81–82

Roman Catholic Church, 14, 59, 60, 157, 161

Rome and Roman Empire (Western Roman Empire), 123f, 138, 149; ancient civilizations, 49–50, 52–53, 54, 54f, 56, 57, 58, *59*, 59–60; migration era (Asia), 66, 71, 83f; modern Europe, 156–58. *See also* Eastern Roman (Byzantine) Empire; Italy

Rouran khaganate (nomadic state), 74, 75

Rule of Law, 178–79, 180, 190–92, 193

Russia, 106f, 110, 111, 112f, 116, 118f, 123f, 135, 185f

Ryukyu Islands, 204

S

Safavid dynasty, 135, 136, 136f, 137, 139, 140, 141, 153, 185f

saigai (north of the Great Wall), 33

sakoku (full national seclusion) (Japan), 170, 174, 202, 204

Samanid dynasty (Iran), 86, 87, 87f, 88, 89

Sasanian dynasty, 50, 56, 60, 66, *66*, 67, 67f, 68, 69, 70, 70f, 73, 85

seiiki (Western Regions), 33, 52, 77

Seiyo shi. See Western historical studies

"Sekaishi josetsu" (A Primer on World History) (Miyazaki), 207–9

self-righteousness, 26–27

Seljuk dynasty, 89, 92, 106f, 110f, 112f, 113, 135, 159f

Sengoku period (Japan), 152, 170, 201

sharia (Islamic system of legal practice), 69

Shatuo (tribe), 94, 95, 96

Shaybanid dynasty, 135

Shia and Shiism (Islamic sect), 85, 86, 89, 113, 114, 136

Shinto, 199, 204

shipbuilding industry, 171–72

Shi Siming, 81–82

Shotoku, Prince (first ruler of unified Japan), 80

Sicily, 157, 158–59, 159f, 160, 161, 162, 163, 165, 168, 176

silk industry, 34, 144, 145, 169, 182, 185f, 201, 202

Silk Road: ancient civilizations, 33–34, 39f, 39–40, *40*, 41, 47, 52, 61; migration era (Asia), 71, 73, 77, 79–80, 85,

90; modern West, 166, 167; Mongol Empire and post-Mongol empires, 121, 122, 130, 133, 140, 149, 150

silver-standard state economies, 167, 168, 173, 174, 183f, 201; early modern Asia, 127, 128, 129, 144, 145, 151, 152, 152f

single-state systems, 96

Sinocentrism, 27, 33, 204

"Sixteen Prefectures of Yan and Yun," 96

Slavs, 54f, 55

Sogdiana, 51, 121, 122, 126, 133; migration era (Asia), 73–74, 76, 77, 85, 86, 88; Turks and Turkic khaganate, 90–91, 92, 92t

Song dynasty, 30, 37f, 61f; achievements of the Mongol Empire, 124, 127, 128, 129, 130, 142, 144; building the Mongol Empire, 105, 106f, 109, 110f, 112f, 115, 117; migration era (Asia), 94, 95, 96–97, 98, 99f, 100; modern West, 171, 176, 179, 189

South Asia, 10, 37, 38, 43, 59, 136f, 140

Southeast Asia, 10, 60, 151, 187

Spain, 167–69, 170, 171, 172, 173f, 174, 175, 181, 185f

spherical earth theory, 166–67

Spring and Autumn and the Warring States periods (China), 52

Sri Lanka, 60, 61f

sugar industry, 173, 173f, 174, 201, 202

Sugiyama Masaaki, 122

Sui dynasty, 37f, 75, 76, 80–81, 82

Sumer, 47

Sunni/Sunnah (orthodox Islamic sect), 85, 113, 114, 137

Syria, 68, 70, 71, 83, 84; ancient civilizations, 48, 49, 50, 56, 59; modern West, 160, 163, 165, 166; Mongol Empire and post-Mongol empires, 114, 117, 118, 137, 149

T

Tamghaji. *See* Zhongyuan

tamya (*tamgha*) ("trade tax"), 127, 129

Tang dynasty, 21, 37f, 63, 121, 149; East/West Asia, 78, 79, 81–82, 83, 83f, 85, 87; maritime empires, 171, 176, 179, 189; migration era (Asia), 74, 75, 75f, 76, *76*, 77; Tang-Song transition, 96–97, 105, 121, 127, 144, 149, 176, 179, 189; Turks and Turkic khaganate, 89, 91, 93, 94, 95

Tang poetry, 63

Tatar Yoke. *See* Mongol Empire and post-Mongol empires

taxation and tax collection, 108, 109, 125–27, 128, 129, 144, 176, 178, 179, 202

tea industry, 145, 169, 182, 185f, 201, 202

Ten Kingdoms (southern China), 94

Teutonic Order, 110, 110f

Theravada Buddhism, 60, 61, 204

Three Kingdoms, 37f, 53

Tibetan Buddhism, 63, 143–44, 147f, 148, 204

Tibet, 99f, 106f, 110f; Tufan, 82, 83f

timber industry, 171–72

Timur (Tamerlane) and Timurid dynasty, 133, 134, 134f, 135, 136, 137, 140, 141, 150, 166

34–35, 35f, 38, 40, 41, 47; formation of, 150, 151, 152f, 153; modern West, 162, 167, 168, 169, 170, 176, 182, 184, 188, 190; "selective systems," 208–9; as understood by Japanese, 13, 14–17, 18–27; as Western history, 10, 11, 12, 22, 206, 207; Western origins of scholarship, 13–16

world religions. *See* Brahmanism; Buddhism; Christianity; Confucianism; Hinduism; Islam; Zoroastrianism

world-systems theory, 11, 16, 19, 173

writing systems, 72, 79, 91, 133, 165, 199, 203; ancient civilizations, 37, 42f, 42–43, 44, 47, 51, 62–63

Wu Zetian, Empress, 80, 81

X

Xianbei tribe. *See* Tuoba clan

Xiao clan, 95

Xiongnu (nomadic state), 74

Xuanzang, 62, *62*

Xuanzong (Tang dynasty), 81

Y

Yamato-kotoba (native Japanese language), 205

Yathrib (Madinat-al-Nabi/City of the Prophet, later Medina), 69

Yazdegerd III (Sasanian dynasty), 68, 70

Yelü Abaoji, 95

Yelü Dashi, 100

yondai bunmei ("four great ancient civilizations"), 41

Yuan dynasty. *See* Dai-ön Yeke Mongol Uls

Yubokumin kara mita sekaishi (Sugiyama), 122

Yungang Grottoes, 61f, 63

yusei kokka (city-states), 31

Z

zamindar ("landowner" or "seigneur") (India), 31

Zheng He, 149

Zhongyuan (central plains), 171; ancient civilizations, 51–52, 53, 56f, 57, 58, 62, 63; migration era (Asia), 79, 80, 81, 82, 83; Mongol Empire and post-Mongol empires, 109, 111, 124, 125, 132, 143; reunification of East/West, 66, 74, 75, 76; as Tamghaji, 77; Turks and Turkic khaganate, 90, 91, 94, 95, 96, 98

Zoroastrianism: ancient civilizations, 50, 51, 58, 60; migration era (Asia), 67, 72, 73, 77

Zuisho Wakokuden (The Book of Sui/ Record of Japan), 80

ABOUT THE AUTHOR

Okamoto Takashi is professor in the Department of Historical Studies, Faculty of Letters, at Kyoto Prefectural University. Born in 1965, he graduated from Kobe University and obtained his Ph.D. in literature from Kyoto University. Okamoto served as associate professor at the University of Miyazaki before assuming his current position, where he specializes in East Asian and modern Asian history. He has published numerous books on modern Asian and Chinese history, of which three have won awards: *Kindai Chugoku to kaikan* [China and the Maritime Customs System in Modern Times] (Nagoya: University of Nagoya Press, 1999), recipient of the Ohira Masayoshi Memorial Prize; *Zokkoku to jishu no aida: Kindai Shin-Kan kankei to Higashi Ajia no meiun* [Between Dependency and Sovereignty: Modern Qing-Korean Relations and the Destiny of East Asia] (Nagoya: University of Nagoya Press, 2004), winner of the Suntory Prize for Social Sciences and Humanities; and *Chugoku no tanjo: Higashi Ajia no kindai gaiko to kokka keisei* [The Birth of China: International Relations and the Formation of a Nation in Modern East Asia] (Nagoya: University of Nagoya Press, 2017), recipient of the Kashiyama Junzo Prize and the Asia-Pacific Prize. Other works available in English include *A World History of Suzerainty: A Modern History of East and West Asia and Translated Concepts* (Tokyo: Toyo Bunko, 2019), for which Okamoto was editor and contributor; and *Contested Perceptions: Interactions and Relations between China, Korea, and Japan since the Seventeenth Century* (Tokyo: JPIC, 2022).

ABOUT THE TRANSLATOR

Following primary Japanese studies at the University of California, Santa Cruz, Michael House has worked in Japan as a Japanese-English translator since 1991. In 2006, he founded the translation company Word House. Prior experience includes patents, IT, and video translation and subtitling.

（英文版）世界史序説：アジア史から一望する
Asia Reoriented: A New Conception of World History

2022 年 6 月 3 日　第 1 刷発行

著　者　岡本隆司
訳　者　ハウス・マイケル
発行所　一般財団法人出版文化産業振興財団
　　　　〒 101-0051 東京都千代田区神田神保町 2-2-30
　　　　電話　03-5211-7283
　　　　ホームページ　https://www.jpic.or.jp/

© 2018 Okamoto Takashi
Printed in Japan
ISBN 978-4-86658-220-7